1000

Days

1000 DAYS

THE MINISTRY OF CHRIST

Jonathan Falwell

THOMAS NELSON
Since 1798

NASHVILLE   DALLAS   MEXICO CITY   RIO DE JANEIRO

Published in Nashville, Tennessee, by Thomas Nelson. Thomas Nelson is a registered trademark of Thomas Nelson, Inc.

Thomas Nelson, Inc., titles may be purchased in bulk for educational, business, fund-raising, or sales promotional use. For information, please e-mail SpecialMarkets@ThomasNelson.com.

Unless otherwise noted, Scripture quotations are taken from the New King James Version®. © 1982 by Thomas Nelson, Inc. Used by permission. All rights reserved.

Scripture quotations marked NIV are from the Holy Bible, New International Version®, NIV®. © 1973, 1978, 1984, 2011 by Biblica, Inc.™ Used by permission of Zondervan. All rights reserved worldwide.

Scripture quotations marked KJV are from the King James Version.

ISBN 978-0-8499-6484-8 (trade paper)

Library of Congress Cataloging-in-Publication Data

Falwell, Jonathan.
  1,000 days : the ministry of Christ / Jonathan Falwell.
     pages cm
Includes bibliographical references.
  ISBN 978-0-8499-4808-4 (hardcover)
1. Christian life. 2. Jesus Christ--Teachings. I. Title.
  BV4501.3.F34 2012
  248.4'861—dc23

                                   2011049518

Printed in the United States of America

CONTENTS

1

WHEN YOU WANT
SOMETHING MORE

About a year ago I watched a documentary about a couple who had devoted their lives to climbing mountains. Reaching the top of peaks was their single driving passion in life, and they were good at it. They had spent years training. They owned all the latest technological gear—air tanks, high tech ropes, ice axes, and crampons. They were muscled and sinewy, and they ate only healthy foods. Every year they planned out their schedules based around which stratosphere-scraping summits they intended to climb—K2, Makalu, Annapurna, and more.

As I watched the show, I found myself respecting what they did. Their lives revolved around a different sort of adventure than most people encounter. This couple traveled to remote corners of the world and scaled the most exotic peaks on the planet. Few live like that, and the couple's story was inspiring, to say the least.

But what got me thinking, what became poignant to me, was when the interviewer began asking the couple about *why* they climbed all these mountains. At that point in the interview, the couple's tone changed and their countenance fell.

"Why do we always climb?" the woman answered the interviewer first. "Because we're always restless."

"We are never satisfied," said the man. "As soon as we climb one peak, we're always unhappy until we can climb another."

I was struck by the unmistakable longing in their voices. As the interview continued, this couple characterized their lives as a constant search. They were no longer climbing for the sheer joy of the sport—it had become a deeper quest; they were climbing because they were searching for purpose. Each expedition became infused with this hunt for meaning. They weren't simply climbing mountains. They were searching for inner peace.

Sorrowfully they admitted they had yet to find what they were looking for. They struggled and sweated and froze and inched their way up the sides of mountains for days and sometimes weeks on end, only to spend a few minutes on top of a mountain before they climbed back down again, shrugged their shoulders, and asked each other, "Well, what's next?"

As I pondered this couple's story, what saddened me was how *many* people's lives are characterized by similar searches, although people might not articulate it just so. In this sense the mountain becomes a metaphor for whatever people think will satisfy their longings for significance, purpose, contentment, and meaning. The act of continually climbing is a metaphor for whatever people try to reach those goals.

I am sure you have encountered this. You can look around at your friends or acquaintances or read news stories about how people are on quests to achieve something, fix something, or obtain something. But the goal is elusive, leaving people dissatisfied. Or if a goal is reached, it often doesn't deliver what was expected. People talk about how they are dissatisfied with their lives, always searching for a greater sense of meaning. Common statements include: "We're always restless," and "We are never satisfied."

Let's make this personal. How about you? Are you climbing mountain after mountain? When you take an honest look at your life, are you yearning for a greater sense of inner peace?

You might not want your life to be *radically* different than it is now; maybe you want it just *a bit* different.

Or perhaps you do indeed want your life to radically change—you can sense that something is deeply skewed, and it is causing you and your loved ones intense pain and sorrow.

Regardless of the degree of change you desire, you can sense that something in your life is not the way it is supposed to be, and you long to satisfy that restless feeling. You want life to work out as you hope it will.

So what's the solution?

You could always climb *another* mountain—whatever your mountain is. You could buy a different car, get a new job, move to a different city, get divorced and remarried, buckle down at work and achieve a promotion, go on another diet, quit your job and try another career, try out a different exercise video, down another drink, buy another outfit, or keep looking to find that perfect someone you had always hoped you would find.

Ask yourself this: How has that worked for you so far?

Think about your current strategy to answer your inner longings. Is that strategy bringing about the satisfaction, peace, fulfillment, and sense of purpose you have been searching for? Are you truly at rest in your inner life? Have you discovered what life is all about, and is it bringing that sense of satisfaction and contentment you have always wanted?

If you can't say yes, then maybe, just maybe . . . the solution is found somewhere else.

THERE MUST BE SOMETHING MORE

The idea of people being on a constant search for inner peace is not a new idea. Hundreds of years ago Saint Augustine described all mankind as having "restless hearts." Augustine understood how we all climb mountain after mountain, always in search of meaning. If you have ever felt a longing for something more, you are not alone.

What might this longing look like in modern life today? Maybe, by all outward appearances, your life seems quite successful. You have a college degree, a solid job, a supportive spouse, and a couple of great kids.

But deep inside you are surprisingly uneasy with how your life has turned out. You know there should be something more to life, but you just can't put your finger on what that is. You might not be able to articulate all the ins and outs of your restlessness, but you catch glimpses of it when you try to answer this longing by buying more stuff—a new phone perhaps, a new shirt, a new car, another carton of ice cream. Or you crank up your schedule and get busier—you begin a new hobby or you fill your calendar to the breaking point, even with good activities like church. No matter how hard you try, nothing satisfies. What do you do?

Or perhaps there is no hiding it—your life is full of chaos. The mistakes you have made are obvious. Your spouse has left, your kids don't talk to you, and you can't hold a job.

Whether the mistakes were caused by you or someone else, you are hurt, and you know you need help. Where do you turn? You've tried self-help books. You've tried Eastern meditation. You've sat through countless support groups. You've searched for solutions everywhere you can think of, but you still feel hopeless. What do you do?

When you long for something more, it can feel as though you are on a constant search for an ideal. You can picture what perfection looks like or tastes like or feels like or sounds like, but you can see that what is in your life now does not line up with perfection. So you are always on the hunt. In the end you are always dissatisfied with what you have because perfection can never be found.

Or sometimes this inner restlessness is like a never-ending search to feel better. Plenty of things regularly occur to shake up a person's life, to give a person a sense of chaos. Perhaps a friend dies of leukemia when she is only thirty-four. Or, frowning, your boss piles up another load of work on your desk right before the start of a weekend. Or it is the end of the month again, and you can't pay all your bills.

Regardless of where your feelings of being shaken originate, there is a very natural tendency to react to that chaotic feeling in not-so-healthful ways in an attempt to immediately feel better. When life gets shaken, people pour another drink or flip to a porn site or go shopping with money that isn't there—all in an effort to feel better. What they really are doing is demonstrating the restlessness of their inner lives.

Restlessness shows up all the time in relationships. People are prone to believe in (and long for) the existence of fairy-tale lives. Somewhere, somehow, the happily-ever-after romances that are seen in the movies must exist. Surely, a person thinks, those relationships can be found if only I could lose some weight, my nose was straighter, I have breast implant surgery, or my significant other would change his bad habits. People look to relationships to satisfy the deep questions within them, longings for answers about life's purpose that go far too deep for another person to ever begin to meet.

Restlessness can show up in our emotions. Sometimes this restlessness emerges at strange times in strange ways. We find ourselves surprised at the sudden fury of anger that emerges when somebody cuts us off on the freeway. Or we can't quite believe how a sad movie could make us cry the way it did. Or we wonder why people are so caustic when they leave comments on a blog posting.

Restlessness shows up in our eating patterns. Often when we reach for another donut or into a bag of potato chips, we are not truly hungry. We eat because we want comfort. Or we are bored. Food has always been there for us. It soothes us. It provides the lift we need to get on with our day or to wind down our evenings.

Restlessness.

Absolutely, it's a common feeling.

Fortunately when Saint Augustine described all mankind as having restless hearts, he didn't leave the subject without pointing toward a solution. The full quote from his book *Confessions* reads this way: "Thou has formed us for Thyself, and our hearts are restless till they find rest in Thee."[1]

That's the solution we want to explore. Rest—an all-encompassing term that means purpose, significance, peace, satisfaction, and an understanding of what is truly important in life. How can our restless hearts be satisfied? How can we end the cycle of always climbing another mountain, whatever our particular mountain may be?

The solution originates with a particular person in a particular stretch of time. When Jesus Christ came to earth more than two thousand years ago, He could have simply offered us salvation—period—and never done another single thing. Jesus could have chosen to be born of a virgin, live for thirty-three years in relative obscurity, die on a cross, be buried, and rise from the dead three days later, and still give us the opportunity for salvation without doing any of the things we read about in the Gospels (the first four books of the New Testament). In actuality the work of salvation was accomplished in one three-day weekend.

Yet there was *more*.

Much more. For three years—roughly 1,000 days—Jesus served in public ministry while on earth. He didn't *need* to provide this ministry, yet He did anyway, and that is the key for us when it comes to rest. This intentionality of Jesus' ministry implies that there is a lot of information in the Scriptures worth grappling with. We need to understand what Jesus said and did during His 1,000-day public ministry so we can apply His teachings to our lives today.

By His modeling in that vitally important three-year stretch of time, Jesus Christ invited us to become like Him—to do similar things, to think similar thoughts, to have similar values, to live lives filled with compassion and justice and fair play and strength of character and sincerity and impartiality and integrity and much more. When we become like Jesus, we can have an incredible impact for what matters. We can also answer the longings in our own hearts. We can glorify God and fulfill our ultimate reason for living.

We can stop climbing mountain after mountain.

We can find true rest.

So Much More to Life than You Think

This is a journey you do not need to take alone. I know what this feeling of restlessness looks like in my own life—and also what it means to answer that feeling of restlessness. I don't know where you are spiritually, if you are a Christian or if you are brand-new to the subject. Either way, I invite you along in the process of discovery.

It is no secret that my dad was a pastor, and that I grew up in a household filled with church activities and faith. I dedicated my life to God when I was six years old, or at least I prayed a prayer toward that aim. I would say the root of my faith was real at a young age, but in many ways I was just punching the card, showing up and doing the things I was supposed to do. Honestly, my faith didn't have much of an impact on me in my early years. It was more a list of dos and don'ts, something I was born into rather than what I was really living. Even though I had a sense of faith, my life was still restless.

Life continued pretty much in that vein until 1989. By then I had been out of college for a few years. One Sunday I was sitting in church. I don't remember what I was thinking about, but my mind definitely wasn't on what was being talked about in the room. I was considering my life. It wasn't great. It wasn't horrible. It was just *okay*. At the time I was working in video and film production, doing TV commercials and wedding videos—nothing earth-shattering, basically just working for a paycheck. My life wasn't falling apart, but there was also an unmistakable emptiness to it. In honest moments I questioned what life was all about. I had friends and family, an okay car, a decent place to live, hobbies, sports, things I enjoyed doing, but I was on an undeniable quest to achieve something, fix something, or obtain something. The goal was ever-elusive for me. I had problems even articulating my restlessness. Try as I might, I found I never achieved, fixed, or obtained what I wanted. The bottom line was I was not satisfied with the way my life was turning out.

But that Sunday morning the pastor invited people to discover Jesus as never before. My mind snapped back to the message. He described how faith must saturate all we do. It is not a list of dos and don'ts, but rather a relationship with a God who cares.

You might call it an *aha* moment. Something clicked in me when he said that, like there was another step to this faith journey beyond praying a prayer or going to church or identifying myself as belonging to a particular group. Nothing beyond that initial realization changed in that moment. I knew there was more journeying ahead for me. The pastor talked about how a call to follow Jesus requires daily steps; it is not a one-time decision. I knew I needed to dig in and find out what these next steps were. So I began to study the teachings of Jesus Christ as never before. I wanted to know this man I knew so little about yet who offered so much hope.

I remember one phrase the pastor said gave me much encouragement—"There's so much more to life than you think." At its core, he explained, life is not about getting things. Or finding yourself. Or about any of the quests you often hear of people pursuing. Rather, the answer to life's longings is found in the true person and work of Jesus Christ.

Without Jesus in our lives—and truly there, not simply by name or intellectual acquiescence—our hearts always will be restless. We always will be unsatisfied with our lives in this world until we find rest in Jesus Christ.

But with Him in our lives, our lives make sense. He is the answer to all our wishes for something more.

Consider this example. Jesus' public ministry was to help us understand what true love is all about—both love for God and love for other people. When we learn to love God and put others first, the rest of life falls into place: our possessions, our ambitions, our hopes, and our dreams. Jesus modeled everything He taught, and His invitation is to make His mission our mission too.

Or consider how Jesus came to provide the ultimate solution to life's problems. When life is spiraling out of control, Jesus said peace can be ours. Jesus came to heal the brokenhearted and to proclaim liberty to those who are bound in addictions. Jesus came to fix what is broken, to heal those people whose lives have been shattered. Jesus is the answer to a marriage that has been ripped apart, to a child who has run away from God, to those who are faced with disease. Whatever the circumstance, He can handle the hurt. Jesus is the answer to everything that might be breaking your heart today. The solution might not quite look like how you imagine it, but it is there, rest assured.

Or consider how Christ invited us to ultimately become like Him. If we are ever searching for what to do in life, for how to find purpose, or for how to live meaningful lives, Jesus answers those questions. When we become like Him, we can have an incredible impact on our communities. The longings of our hearts are satisfied. We glorify God and fulfill our ultimate reason for living. We are fulfilled in being able to shine His light around us on earth.

Whether you already know Jesus Christ or are just exploring who He is, this book offers the opportunity for you to meet with Jesus Christ like never before. It is a journey to understand His teachings, model your life after His example, and follow Him in a new way. It is a call to find satisfaction in the person of Jesus Christ and to live for Him.

My heart has found an answer to its restlessness in the person of Jesus Christ, and I know you can find this same peace and purpose too.

In the pages ahead what we want to do is truly get a sense of what it is that Jesus wants us to know about what He did, what He said, who He is, and what He wants us to do about that. Constantly we will be asking the questions: How does this impact us? How might this change who we are?

It would be impossible within this book to look at everything the Gospels record about what Jesus did during His roughly 1,000 days of ministry on earth, so we have created additional resources for you that can be found at this website: http://1000days.trbc.org. Here you will find videos and extra teachings about a variety of aspects of the life of Christ. There is a section called "100-Day Reading" that will help guide you through all four Gospels for yourself. If you use Twitter, click the button called "@ChristSays." Every day you will receive an example of something Christ said that can apply to your life. If you want to do additional independent study on the life of Christ, there are four navigation buttons: "Key Groups," "Key People," "Key Places," and "Key Events."

Yes, a study on the 1,000 days of Jesus' ministry does take commitment on our part. If we are willing to stop and listen to the words of Christ, His teachings will take us from a place of emptiness and confusion to a place of peace that goes beyond human comprehension.

Jesus did not promise us a life free from trouble. He is called the

God of all comfort—and if there were no troubles, He would not need to be called by this name. Jesus does not promise freedom from all problems, but He does promise that we will never face situations alone.

Wisdom from the Zip Line

Why should we listen to Jesus?

Because He knows what He's talking about. He's the author of life.

Last summer my wife and I and our four school-age children took a trip to the beach. One day it rained and there was nothing to do. We saw an ad in the hotel lobby for a zip line adventure about forty-five minutes away, so we decided to give it a try. We drove over to the site, and they gave us a safety lesson; then we all climbed a tower that seemed a hundred feet tall.

One by one each member of my family got strapped into this contraption, then leapt from the tower and whizzed down the zip line, shouting and laughing and screaming.

My son Nicholas, who was ten at the time, wanted to go last. When his turn came, however, he chose not to go.

"I just don't want to do this," he said when I asked him why.

"It's completely safe," I said, "and a lot of fun. Are you sure you don't want to try?"

"Well, maybe I'll do it," he said.

The operator hooked Nicholas up again. He crept toward the edge of the tower, then stopped and shook his head. "Nope!" Nicholas said again. "I changed my mind. I'm not going to do this."

Again I went up and talked with Nicholas. Again I reassured him that everything would be fine. Again he crept to the edge of the tower. Again he backed out at the last minute.

A third time I talked to him. A third time he agreed to try. A third time he changed his mind and refused to jump.

By now people behind us in line were getting exasperated. I didn't know what else to do. I knew that Nicholas would have a great time on the zip line if he would only try. No matter what I said, Nicholas just wouldn't agree to take the leap that his mother, brother, and sisters had already taken. At that moment I glanced out of the corner of my eye and saw the operator walk over to Nicholas and whisper in his ear.

Nicholas nodded his head.

And—very suddenly—he jumped!

Nicholas shouted and laughed and whizzed down the zip line. When he got to the bottom, I ran over to congratulate him.

"Hey!" I said. "That was great! But I'm curious—what did the operator say that made you change your mind?"

"Uh, he just told me everything would be okay," Nicholas said.

"But I've been telling you the exact same thing for the past thirty minutes. Why did you listen to him and not me?"

Nicholas grinned. "Because the guy knows what he's talking about."

In all seriousness this is why it is so important to listen to the Source of all truth, to Jesus Christ. So much of the time we are not listening to Jesus—and that is what causes all our restlessness. But Jesus knows the answer to life, and a few words from the guy who knows what He is talking about can make all the difference in life.

This book studies the person at the heart of all answers. It represents the opportunity for you to meet Jesus Christ as never before. This book is a journey to know His teachings and example and grow to love and serve Him in a new way.

If you have found yourself grappling with a restless heart, what follows is a journey that can give you true rest—that all-encompassing term that means purpose, significance, peace, and an understanding of what is truly important.

This is the promise: Jesus will set you free from a life of dissatisfaction.

He will answer the longings of your heart.

QUESTIONS FOR INDIVIDUAL REFLECTION
OR SMALL GROUP DISCUSSION

1. Have you ever seen an instance where people undertake a certain activity (perhaps with great passion) because there's an unmistakable longing in their inner lives? What was it like?

2. Saint Augustine said, "Thou has formed us for Thyself, and our hearts are restless till they find rest in Thee." How have you seen this quote to be true in your own life—whether your heart is still restless, or whether you have found rest in God?

3. Jonathan talked about how his faith began to get real for him when he discovered that there was "another step to this faith journey beyond praying a prayer or going to church or identifying [himself] as belonging to a particular group." What was that additional step? Have you experienced something similar in your own life?

4. Jesus has been described as "the author of life" (Acts 3:15 NIV). What does this mean?

5. In your most honest moments, where are you spiritually right now, and where do you want to be?

JESUS CLOSE-UP

I magine you are on a long hike.

Not a hike to climb mountain after mountain but just a good, long hike at a nearby wilderness area. Sweat pours down your face, and your muscles quiver. It is a record-hot day, and you have been trekking in that heat very hard. Your throat is dry, and your lips are cracked. The sun is a merciless disc overhead, and panic rises in your throat as you feel dizziness coming on. Relief seems only something to dream about.

But suddenly you are at the brink of a clear mountain pool of sparkling water. You hesitate only to shed the boots and backpack, and you take the plunge. Ahhh. Down into the cool depths, up till the water breaks over your head and sprays around you, you can't help laughing. Instantly you feel revived, refreshed, and full of energy. Invigorated, you explore the pool. The coolness reaches your core. You revel in its effect on your body and soul. Suddenly you know you can get back on the trail.

In fact, you can do more than merely put one foot in front of the other on the trail. Now that you have immersed yourself deeply in the restorative power of that pool, you can hike with new enthusiasm. It is no longer about drudgery, toil, and frustration. It's about exhilaration in the journey; it's about freedom to explore and about excitement in what is around the next bend in the trail. Because of the refreshment of the plunge, you have found new liberty, energy, and joy. You see clearly where you are going and why, and you know you will make it. There is a new spark to the journey and joy in the destination. That plunge was as good as a rest.

That is what I am inviting you to do in this book: take the plunge. We live in an age and culture where we feel as though we are on a long hike. Often the hike is exciting, but many times it fries our minds, drains us of spiritual energy, saps our strength, and threatens to flatten us altogether. The answer is to plunge into something that will indeed get us up and going in the direction our Creator intended. We need to immerse ourselves into something that will energize and equip us to impact our barren culture.

As we plunge into the life of Jesus, delving into those three key years of His ministry as explained in the first chapter, we will try to get a sense of how the pattern of His life can change the pattern of ours as His followers.

Jesus spent so much time walking the dusty roads of this earth and living among us in ways that must have been humiliating for the King of glory. Why didn't He just get right to the point? We understand that Jesus came to save us. He was born to die. Bethlehem, the place where Jesus was born, points to Calvary, the place where He was crucified. We get that. It's the foundation of the Christian faith, the driving force behind every program of Christian mission.

So why did Jesus bother doing anything else? Could Jesus simply have fast-forwarded from Bethlehem straight to the cross? Could He have skipped the parables, the one-on-one conversations where He patiently dialogued with individuals, the Sermon on the Mount, the walking on water, the miraculous picnics for crowds? None of it was really necessary in providing salvation.

But He did all these things to show us a way of life that is absolutely vital if we want to find rest for our inner longings. It's not about salvation; it's about truly becoming the God-followers He intends us to be. It's about finding His purpose for us and thus satisfaction for our inner restlessness. He knows that comes about as we become more like Him. So He's showing us Himself in a journey of 1,000 days. As we plunge into those 1,000 days, listen to Him saying simply, "Watch Me."

LEADING UP TO THE 1,000 DAYS

When two of my kids, Jonathan and Jessica, had science exams recently, I had the privilege of quizzing them on certain facts as they prepared to take their tests. Many facts we learn while in school tend to fall out of our minds as we grow older, so it was a joy to be reminded again about some of the particulars of creation. My kids and I talked about how the earth is hung in space and set at the perfect tilt of 23.4 degrees, which creates the seasons we enjoy. The tilt and gravity all work together to control the spin and make for a planet that is hospitable to life.

Before God created the universe and set it into motion, He planned to someday personally enter into His creation. He planned to target planet Earth to provide a way to bring us back into relationship with Him, and we are told He had each one of us in mind. At a specific point in time and at a particular place, He began this mission of mercy.

God stepped into human history on a tiny piece of real estate at the edge of the Mediterranean Sea, a little sliver of the world called Israel, a place about 55 miles wide and 130 miles from north to south. All Christ's ministry, everything recorded in the Bible about His earthly life, took place on that little strip of land, except one brief journey when Joseph and Mary took the infant Jesus to Egypt to escape from King Herod who was out to kill babies. God the Son stepped into the human experience at a specific region of Israel, Judea, into a meager little city called Bethlehem. The one who created it all actually entered into the creation.

It gets very personal as God interacts with individuals, ordinary people like you and me. At the beginning of Luke's record in the Bible, we see God the Son poised on the edge of time and space to enter creation and begin His journey. A young woman, Mary, is approached by an angel who tells her not to be afraid, but she is to understand that she will conceive a child, will give birth to a son, and is to name Him Jesus. The angel tells her several amazing things about this child: He will be great, the Son of the Highest, and the

Lord God will give Him the throne of His ancestor David. He will reign over the house of Jacob forever and His kingdom will never end. (Read the record in Luke 1:30–33.)

Put yourself in Mary's shoes. Can you imagine what must have been going through her mind when an angel told her all this? Actually, she protested. "This is impossible," she basically said, "because I am a virgin. There is no way that I can have a child."

The angel assured her, "With God nothing will be impossible" (Luke 1:37). If you were Mary, wouldn't you wonder about this? A virgin is to bear a child who will be God, who will own an ancient throne and reign forever? Incredible as it sounds, it is not impossible because with God all things are possible. And so it happened.

The Bible tells us little about Jesus' infancy and childhood. The next focal point comes when He is twelve years old, a story told in Luke 2. Joseph and Mary took Jesus along as they visited Jerusalem for the Passover feast. A day into their journey home, they realized that Jesus was no longer with them. You can imagine that, as parents, they were scared to death. They ran back to Jerusalem to look for Him.

For three days they searched until they finally laid eyes on Him.

Luke 2:46–47 says, "They found Him in the temple, sitting in the midst of the teachers, both listening to them and asking them questions. And all who heard Him were astonished at His understanding and answers."

When they found Him, Mary spoke words that are familiar to parents everywhere: "Son, why have You done this to us? Look, Your father and I have sought You anxiously" (Luke 2:48). We probably would have said, "Young man, where have you been? Don't you know that you have scared us to death?" I mean, we would not have been happy.

A couple of years ago our family was at Disney World. Somehow Jessica wandered off to look at something and disappeared from our view. We couldn't find her anywhere. Man, it scared me to death. We ran around looking for her everywhere. Finally we found her, and I said something similar to what Mary said, something like, "Where have you been?! Why have you done this?!"

Jesus' answer may surprise us. He said, "Why did you seek Me? Did you not know that I must be about My Father's business?" (Luke 2:49). If Jessica had said that, she wouldn't have been able to sit down for a week. But for Jesus, such an answer was correct and respectful because He had the authority. All those gathered in that temple, hearing His words, were astonished that this twelve-year-old knew so much. They were amazed at His wisdom and authority.

We've had a glimpse of Jesus' person as the angel spoke to Mary as well as a glimpse of His wisdom and authority in the temple. Now we will get a glimpse of His mission. Move forward eighteen years. Jesus is about thirty years old when we see the next scene in His life. He had traveled to the Jordan River to meet John the Baptist, a story told in Matthew 3. Jesus approached John and asked to be baptized. You can imagine John saying, "Whoa, wait a minute. I don't need to baptize You. I mean, I'm not worthy." But Jesus pressed the point. John obeyed and plunged Jesus into the Jordan in the ceremony of baptism. When Jesus came up from the water, the skies opened and the Spirit of God descended in the form of a dove and lighted upon Him. A voice spoke from heaven, saying, "This is My beloved Son, in whom I am well pleased" (Matt. 3:17).

At that moment Jesus said to you and me across the years of history, "Watch Me. Watch closely." At that moment Jesus began His ministry. From His first thirty years we are told only about His arrival on earth, His time in the temple at age twelve, and the baptism that launched His ministry. There are eighty-nine chapters in the four gospel stories—Matthew, Mark, Luke, and John. Only four chapters deal with Jesus' first thirty years. Most days during those thirty years He was probably doing things similar to what we do in our early years, only He was probably doing it a lot better than we do. He was busy growing up, spending time with His mom, and working with His dad. The Bible record is mostly silent about those thirty years. But then His ministry kicked into gear. At age thirty His 1,000 days of ministry began.

Launch of the 1,000 Days

The culture in which Christ launched His ministry would look very familiar to us. It was filled with broken hearts, people chained and addicted to various unhealthy things, the blind leading the blind, people abused and oppressed and crushed and suffering injustice. Certainly that describes people in our society, probably people whom you know and interact with. Maybe it describes you, and you long for a way out or around or through these situations and frustrations. You may long for a way to impact our society in positive ways and fulfill the mission of Christ for your life today. Yet you feel caught in a culture that can accurately be pictured as a barren desert.

In this same kind of milieu, Jesus launched His ministry in His hometown of Nazareth. He went to the synagogue as was His pattern. Picture a synagogue of that day: it was much like churches of today in that it was a place where people came together to study God's Word. The synagogue was a square stone structure, placed in the middle of the community. Inside, three or four tiers of seats were built around the square. People looked toward the middle, where there was a central table holding a scroll of the Word of God.

During the week the synagogue was the social center. Even the school met here. On the Sabbath day, the holy day, people came there to worship God. The ruler of the synagogue determined the content and order of service. Plans were laid four or five years in advance. The ruler decided who would do the readings and kept everything on schedule and proper. If a traveling rabbi came to the synagogue, he would be asked to read the scripture. People sang psalms together, prayed, and recited Deuteronomy 6:4: "The LORD is one." Then the scroll was opened, read, and interpreted.

When Jesus walked into the building that day, the same synagogue where He had grown up, the ruler of the synagogue recognized Him as the visiting rabbi and invited Him to read the scripture. Remember, that scripture passage had been chosen four or five years earlier. Jesus was handed the scroll of Isaiah 61, and with this scripture He announced His ministry. This is what He read:

The Spirit of the LORD is upon Me, because He has anointed Me to preach the gospel to the poor; He has sent Me to heal the broken-hearted, to proclaim liberty to the captives and recovery of sight to the blind, to set at liberty those who are oppressed; to proclaim the acceptable year of the LORD. (Luke 4:18–19, quoting from Isa. 61:1–2)

A hush probably fell over the room as He rolled up the scroll, gave it back to the attendant beside the table in the center of the room, and sat down. Every eye was fixed on Jesus. How would He interpret what He had just read? He said, "Today this Scripture is fulfilled in your hearing" (Luke 4:21).

The words must have fallen like a bombshell in the room. Jesus was saying, "That's Me." The Messiah that Isaiah and other prophets promised would come, the One who would bring redemption and hope, satisfaction and rest—that's Me. Jesus chose that small group in His hometown synagogue to announce, "I am the Messiah. I am the One who will do all those things Isaiah wrote about. This scripture is being fulfilled in your hearing."

His mission was announced. It would spill out from that little synagogue and spread into the streets of Nazareth, move out from Nazareth throughout the nation of Israel and eventually around the world, even to your town and your street. The mission that started in the Nazareth synagogue is the mission we are about today. The way Jesus would impact His barren culture is the way we are to impact ours. His mission of mercy is to be our focus too.

Yes, Jesus could have chosen to skip those three itinerant years, but He chose to immerse Himself in 1,000 days of intensive ministry. He wanted to showcase some things for you and me to pay particular attention to that He knew we'd need in our journeys. He wanted to ensure that we would apply the things He said and did into our own lives, and allow Him to do the same things through us. In a sense He showcased Himself during these three years so our lives could become the extension of His life. Sound impossible? After all, He was the Son of God, He owned the throne of David, and His kingdom would never end. Add to that: the Spirit of God was upon Him. How can we possibly live the kind of life He lived? Look ahead to the book of Acts and you'll see that just before Jesus went back to heaven He promised we, too, would receive power when the Holy Spirit came. The same Spirit of God that was with Jesus is with us, and for the same mission.

Unpacking the Mission

Let's plunge more deeply into those words of Jesus where He described His mission. This speaks to our deepest needs, to what He wants to do in us and through us to our world. Did you notice He referred specifically to four groups: the poor, brokenhearted, captives, and blind? These are the folks who people our neighborhoods, who rub shoulders with us at work, who sit in our pews, who look back at us from our mirrors.

Jesus said He came to preach the gospel to the poor. That word *poor* in the original language means "destitute, impoverished, with absolutely nothing." That is how every one of us enters this world, and you may still be in that condition. We are not talking about having no money or possessions but about being poor in spirit, having no hope, no joy, and nothing for which to live. Jesus came to change that, to give good news of redemption and hope to those impoverished in spirit.

Jesus turned to the brokenhearted. Do you know any people with broken hearts? How about your own? This week I talked to a family who had lost a ten-year-old child. Now that's brokenheartedness. I have sat with families waiting in the hospital, only to hear the doctors tell them there is no hope for their loved one. I have stood with many at gravesides. There are a lot of broken hearts. Jesus embraced the brokenhearted with compassion. He did many things during His 1,000 days of ministry aimed at healing the brokenhearted, offering them hope.

Jesus went on to say that He came to proclaim liberty to captives. The word *captive* to us implies someone who has been locked up, maybe incarcerated. That is too limiting for what Jesus meant. He was referring to all those who are bound. In today's world Satan is working at binding us all, trying to get us caught up by sin, shackled in its chains. You may be captive to alcoholism or drug addiction or pornography. Or perhaps you jump from relationship to relationship, always hoping to find a solid kind of love. Maybe some secret thing has a grip on you and you feel that you dare not tell anyone. It's possible to be captive to anything that wraps around and holds you back from being the person God created you to be. There is no program or self-help book or group you can join that will ultimately set you free. Only the power of God can do it. He may use human tools, but the real work of setting captives free is a God-work. Jesus proclaimed liberty.

Jesus didn't forget the blind and how desperately they need recovery of sight. If you have ever had trouble with your eyesight, you know how frightening that can be. If you have worn a blindfold as a child and played pin the tail on the donkey, you understand just a little of the experience. If you have gone down deep into a cave into complete darkness, you know how lost you can feel.

A woman who gradually lost her eyesight as an adult gamely studied all the helps she could get and coped with her situation with the aid of a specially trained guide dog. She wisely chose a career in which the use of her hands was more important than the use of her eyes and became a physiotherapist. She admitted one of her hardest experiences came when she realized that losing her sight meant becoming illiterate. She could no longer read or write. We often forget how many other losses go along with the loss of sight.

You can see the parallels. If you are spiritually blind, you grope in sin's darkness and the loneliness of being lost and directionless. You can't even read directions to get out. But Jesus offers recovery of sight. We can expect it to be a lifelong process. Even after we are saved, Jesus keeps on giving us more and more spiritual vision.

In Luke 4:18, Jesus summarized His mission: "To set at liberty those who are oppressed." The Greek translation of the original Hebrew for *oppressed* is the word *thrau-oh*. It means one who has been "bruised or broken, shattered into pieces." Jesus came to fix what is broken, shattered, and torn apart. Even if that's you.

Remember, Jesus said all these things in the hometown synagogue, in that little square room with every eye fixed on Him. After the hush, after the shock, after a little discussion among the people, what happened next was like an explosion. The people in that room rose up to do to Jesus what all the world tries to do to Him, what all of us have done in our hearts. They became furious. They worked themselves into frenzy, drove Him out of town, dragged Him to the brow of a hill, and tried to throw Him over the cliff. They wanted to destroy the man who proposed to take them out of their comfort zones. They rejected His words and tried to get rid of Him. But it was not Jesus' time to die, and He was in control. The record says He walked right through the crowd and went on His way. He had places to go, things to do.

He had a ministry to launch for us.

YOUR CHOICE TODAY

As we begin our journey through the 1,000 days of Christ's ministry, we each need to ask, what am I going to do with this message, this mission? We can choose to reject it or receive it. How would it look to receive it?

Maybe you are one of the brokenhearted, one of the oppressed or shattered, or you feel smashed into pieces. Jesus' words to you are this: "I'm here to set you free." You may be trapped in sin, desperate to be free. You may be caught up in brokenness, your whole life splintered, and your heart ripped apart. You don't know the way out. But Jesus did what He did and said what He said to give you freedom. There is nothing gripping you today that is greater than the power of Jesus in your life.

Maybe you are one of the comfortable. You are a God-follower, a genuine Christian, but you really don't want to get out of your seat. You don't want to share your faith. The mission scares you or simply doesn't interest you. You, too, have a choice to make. Your invitation is to travel that road with Jesus. His words for you, too, are: "I'm here to set you free," free from your fear and your lethargy.

Take a moment to focus on the decision before you. There is an old hymn that invites you to "turn your eyes upon Jesus, look full in his wonderful face."[1] That is where your answer lies.

May I suggest that as you continue reading this book, you read not simply to see what it says but with a commitment to take the plunge. Dive into the life of Christ and explore it and find your restlessness satisfied in Him. Let His life impact your barren heart, and it will also impact your barren culture. Jesus *is* the answer. His invitation is to make His mission your mission. And to make His rest your rest.

Questions for Individual Reflection or Small Group Discussion

1. We live in a culture that can fry our minds, drain us of our spiritual energy, sap our strength, and threaten to flatten us altogether. How have you seen this to be evident in your own life?

2. Read Luke 4:16–21. What did Jesus mean when He said, "Today this Scripture is fulfilled in your hearing"?

3. How does Jesus' mission speak to our deepest needs, to what He wants to do in us and then through us for our world?

4. "Jesus proclaims liberty to captives." What does this mean? Who are the captives? What might they be held captive to? And what does liberty look like?

5. "Jesus is the answer." What does this mean in your life?

3

ORDINARY PEOPLE, EXTRAORDINARY LIVES

A story is told about George and Carol, a married couple who were university students during the late 1950s. They were kind and good people, but fairly average, not people you would notice as exceptional. Their backgrounds were basic. They did not ace the academic world. They were never chosen as most likely to succeed in the school's yearbook, nor did they ever wear homecoming crowns. Neither was exceptionally good-looking. They could even be described as plodders. They worked persistently to get in assignments on time, although they didn't rack up A grades. They never failed to show up at their part-time jobs and do their duties. George struggled especially with foreign languages but slogged away at verbs until he mastered them. Carol was daunted by public speaking but followed instructions and managed to fulfill requirements. In short, they were ordinary people. But they developed excellent work habits and committed themselves to faithfulness. When they gave their word, you could count on it.

Fast-forward more than half a century. George and Carol, unlike some of their more impressive classmates, had not washed out. They were still married to each other. They were still serving God on the mission field where He had sent them. They had translated most of the New Testament into a language that previously had none of God's Word, a task where the ability to plod was a strong asset. When retirement age came and went, George and Carol didn't stop. They went to another foreign field, established a new mission, and learned a new language. They took on challenges that would have daunted people half their age, such as writing for international newspapers, helping government officials negotiate tricky situations, and living the life of good neighbors in a land where soldiers toted rifles on every street corner. The plodders had become triumphantly successful. The ordinary folks had become extraordinarily used by God.

How does this happen? How does God take ordinary people and make them extraordinary?

Maybe you feel as though your life is nothing special. Perhaps you are a plodder, or you have no special skills, or you don't know the right people, or you are not outstanding in anything, or you are just not good enough or proficient enough or powerful enough to make any significant impact for God. Or perhaps you evaluate your life as damaged goods. Because of past mistakes or grievous sin patterns or victimization, you feel irreparably scarred. You may feel you have blown it so badly that God has placed you on a shelf. You may feel doomed to a life of restless nonfulfillment.

Is it possible for God to take your life and make it count for eternity?

Can God do anything with you?

ZEROING IN ON SOME ORDINARY PEOPLE

In the last chapter we looked at how Jesus spent 1,000 days in intensive ministry to show us how His life can become transformative for us. We saw who it really was who lay in the Bethlehem manger, God the Son stepping into human history; we saw His wisdom and authority grip people in the temple when He was twelve, and we saw His mission launched at the Jordan River when He was thirty. Besides His main mandate to die in payment for our sins, Jesus described His mission as targeting four groups: the poor, brokenhearted, captives, and blind.

Now we come to the Sea of Galilee. This was a locale where He would find plenty of poor, brokenhearted, captive, and blind people. Jesus spent massive amounts of time in His earthly ministry in this small region. When we think of the word *sea*, we picture large bodies of water like the Mediterranean Sea or even the Caribbean Sea. But in comparison, the Sea of Galilee was nothing more than a lake. It was about thirteen miles north to south and about eight miles east to west. It was sometimes referred to as the Lake of Gennesaret because of a fertile region called Gennesaret that lay on the western slopes of the sea.

This tiny area becomes hugely important in the ministry of Jesus. In this region are the towns of Capernaum, where Jesus healed Peter's mother-in-law; Magdala, the place Mary Magdalene called home; and Caesarea Philippi, where Jesus said to Peter, "On this rock I will build My church" (Matt. 16:18). On the western shores Jesus cast out demons from a man and into pigs. The herd ran down the hill and into the water. (I have always wanted to go scuba diving there to see if we can find pig bones in that area.) On the slopes of this Galilee shoreline, Jesus preached the Sermon on the Mount. All these dramatic events happened around the Sea of Galilee.

In the Sea of Galilee we find eighteen types of indigenous fish. If you enjoy fishing, you can appreciate that fact. The first story in the Bible that deals with the Sea of Galilee is about fishing. It is found in Luke 5. Here Jesus first meets some ordinary people who become extraordinary. He is going to call them to just walk away from everything they ever knew and to follow Him.

A crowd of people pressed around Jesus one day trying to hear as He taught the Word of God. He noticed two small boats at the water's edge and fishermen nearby washing their nets. Jesus climbed into one boat, which happened to belong to a man called Simon (whom Jesus would soon after rename Peter). Jesus asked Simon to shove out a little way from shore and anchor the boat. Then Jesus used the boat as a pulpit, a platform from which to speak to the people without being crowded too closely.

When Jesus finished His teaching, He told Simon to launch out into deep water and let down the net for a catch. Simon was a little reluctant, saying they had been working all night and had caught nothing. In Simon's opinion it just didn't seem to be a good day for fishing. If you are a fisherman, you can understand that he was saying, "Man, we've been out there trying, but we haven't even had a bite. No luck. It's a waste of time to try again." Still Simon must have been impressed with something about Jesus as he continued, "Okay, in spite of everything, because You say so, I'll let down the net again" (v. 5).

Before long they had caught so many fish the net threatened to break. Simon and his brother Andrew signaled their partners in the second boat, James and John, to come and help. Soon they had both boats so full of fish they were in danger of sinking. Simon got it then; he knew Jesus was someone special and he was someone ordinary. He fell on his knees and called Jesus "Lord" and called himself a "sinful man."

Notice the reaction in Luke 5:9–11:

For he and all who were with him were astonished at the catch of fish which they had taken; and so also were James and John, the sons of Zebedee, who were partners with Simon. And Jesus said to Simon, "Do not be afraid. From now on you will catch men." So when they had brought their boats to land, they forsook all and followed Him.

I wonder if we can grasp the impact of this anomaly in their routine. These were men who every single day of their adult lives would step into their boats, take them into the middle of the Sea of Galilee, and try to catch a few of those eighteen different types of fish that make this sea their home. Centuries later, people are still doing this. If you travel there today, you can still see the boats going out every morning to catch fish. If you go to a Galilee restaurant you can see that prominent on the menu is something called "St. Peter's Fish."

Now let me warn you: this is a disgusting experience. A server brings you a big platter and sets it down in front of you. The fish still has all the scales, fins, and the tail. The big fish eyes are looking at you. The mouth sits halfway open. And the waiter says, "Enjoy!"

That's when I went looking for the McDonald's I had heard was located in the basement of a hotel in Tiberias.

But today, just as long ago, people fish in Galilee and sell the fish to provide for their families. People have been doing it day after day, season after season, lifetime after lifetime, century after century. For Simon and his partners it must have seemed routine, ordinary, and sometimes pointless. Maybe that is the way your days feel too. The routine that has fallen to you might feel unimportant and pointless. You are walking on some kind of treadmill and getting nowhere. So you can identify with Simon and his companions. You are longing for something more. An inner restlessness drives you to seek fulfillment and purpose and significance.

It was these ordinary, discouraged, hardworking, restless people whom Jesus invited to follow Him that day. After seeing Him produce a miraculous load of fish in their nets, they left it all behind upon hearing His call and followed Him. We see clearly that Jesus chose common people. That is so encouraging, that He chose people like you and me to follow after Him and to serve Him.

Get that key phrase strongly into your mind: "They forsook all and followed Him" (Luke 5:11).

There is a greater purpose for our existence than merely getting up every morning and going to work, only to come home at the end of the day, sleep, and do it all over again. Jesus invites us to participate with Him in His mission. This invitation is for everyone—no matter our age, gender, race, skills, or occupation. Following Jesus is what life is truly about.

WHY NOT CHOOSE THE MOVERS AND SHAKERS?

It was no small task to which Jesus called these fishermen when He invited them to follow Him. Yes, then and now, it was about personal satisfaction, but more, it's about changing the world. For such a crucial job, it seems strange to call ordinary, simple people. There's no question that Jesus could have chosen the religious leaders of the day.

He could have called Pharisees and Sadducees or some of the priests who were in charge of the temple. Or He could have called politically powerful people, jet-setters, or that day's equivalent of rock stars or sports icons. That always gets attention. Instead, Jesus chose some uneducated laborers who would not be seen by their community as world-changers in any sense.

A clue to Jesus' thinking is found in 1 Corinthians 1:26–27:

> For you see your calling, brethren, that not many wise according to the flesh, not many mighty, not many noble, are called. But God has chosen the foolish things of the world to put to shame the wise, and God has chosen the weak things of the world to put to shame the things which are mighty.

The key phrase is in verse 29: "that no flesh should glory in His presence." One strong reason that He chose ordinary people is so no one could brag. No one could boast of being some kind of plum that God was lucky to get.

We see people getting it all backward, even today. Recently a great intellectual scientist, certainly brilliant and influential, stated that creation could have happened without God, just spontaneously. He admitted he doesn't believe in the existence of a personal God. Although this man has done much for the world of science that is truly valuable, his statement shows that even if people are highly educated and brilliant, they do not always get it right.

When I heard about his statement, I remembered God's words in 1 Corinthians 1:26–27. God chooses simple people to put down the arrogance of the powerful who deny Him. Aren't you glad that God chose people like you and me? There are those who think they have all the answers, but ordinary people can share the gospel message and trump all false intellectualism.

Let's look more closely at the twelve men Jesus called to follow Him and be His closest friends and disciples. Maybe we will see in their lives some of the same things we see in our own lives.

FOCUSING ON THE FOLLOWERS

That Jesus chose these people to be His followers flies in the face of conventional wisdom. Take a look at Peter, for instance. He's a rough-around-the-edges kind of guy, constantly sticking his foot in his mouth. He certainly lacked wisdom, yet Jesus called him.

Simon Peter's brother Andrew was also called to follow. Andrew was a people pleaser, really just a behind-the-scenes kind of guy, quite a contrast to his brother. Yet he was often shown bringing people to the Savior.

James, the son of Zebedee, battled with pride. Later on in the story he demands to sit beside Christ on His right hand when the kingdom is established. But despite James's pride, Jesus chose him to be one of His disciples.

John, brother of James, was known for youthful immaturity. Philip was a guy who lived by the book. Bartholomew was a brilliant man, an intellectual, a theological thinker.

Thomas is one of the better-known disciples, but what is he known for? Doubting. He's the guy who doubted everything. He battled with trust issues, including trusting Jesus Himself.

Matthew was a tax collector, a financial genius who probably had been in the process of selling his soul to cheat his countrymen when Jesus stepped in and called him. Matthew was such a contrast to Peter. Today we would probably see Peter in a blue-collar job, maybe with antlers hanging in his family room above his TV and a shotgun over the back window of his pickup. Matthew was probably on the other side of the spectrum. Today he would probably be a left-wing radical who wants to take every dollar you have. It's interesting to see that Jesus called people from all walks of life to forsake all and follow Him, and He expected them to get along together in the mission He would give them.

James, son of Alphaeus, was a person who lived in obscurity with no desire for fame and fortune. Thaddeus was unimpressive in stature and youthfulness. Simon the Zealot was downright scary, extremely passionate, unbridled, and maybe a little crazy. Then there was Judas

Iscariot. His story is one of the best known but for all the wrong reasons. He was the one who focused on love of money, who became the betrayer.

In Luke 8 we read the story of Mary Magdalene, at first possessed by demons, but Jesus called her out of that. Joanna, in a key position as the wife of the manager of Herod's household, and Susanna were two women Jesus called, who became financial supporters of the work.

Some of the stories of these followers of Jesus might sound familiar to you. Maybe you are a rough-around-the edges person like Peter or a background person like Andrew. Perhaps you battle pride or immaturity or bring a lot a bad baggage from your past. You could have trust issues or might come from some brand of radical extremism. Maybe you are just brokenhearted, shattered by what life has handed you, starved in your spirit, addicted to unhealthy things, blind to Jesus' love. Just like these people, you are invited to hear Jesus' call to follow Him.

THE ESSENCE OF THE CALL

Remember Jesus told the fishermen He called away from their old lives that they would become fishers of men. The call came on the heels of the biggest catch of fish that Peter, Andrew, James, and John had probably ever seen. For those of you who like fishing, can you imagine going out and bringing back so many that your boat nearly sinks? Or hauling in record-size king salmon? That would be a pretty good day, don't you think? You'd be pumped to go again.

But Luke 5:11 says, "When they had brought their boats to land, they forsook all and followed Him."

The Greek word translated *forsook* is *ah-fee-a-mee*. The definition is literally "to drop what is in your hands," walk away, and leave it behind. Peter and his partners turned their backs on a pile of fish that was probably more than they had ever seen in one place. They stepped out of those boats and dropped the nets and just left the catch right there. (Probably the nearby poor people had a windfall that day.)

Peter and his friends set their courses to follow Jesus. They left it all to follow Him.

When Mark told the story in his gospel, he said they didn't wait. They dropped everything immediately. No standing around weighing pros and cons. James and John stepped out of the boat and left their father behind and followed after Jesus, with no idea what the road ahead would look like, no idea what kinds of issues they would face, what kinds of problems they would go through, or what difficulties lay ahead. In fact, Jesus told them that they would be persecuted. Some would die because of following Him. Yet they dropped the nets and followed Him with absolute faith, pure trust, complete courage, their eyes affixed.

WHAT DOES THIS LOOK LIKE FOR US?

One day my kids and I headed to Wintergreen, a nearby ski resort. It was a great day, awesome weather. Now, I hadn't skied in twenty-five years. In fact, the last time I skied, I broke my leg. But I was looking forward to this. Jonathan Jr., Jessica, Natalie, Nicholas, and I grabbed our skis and headed out. We had a blast.

At one point Natalie and I were riding up the ski lift and happened to glance at the booth where you rent skis and buy tickets. There was a guy putting on skis and an orange vest. On the vest were two words: *Blind Skier.* In my mind those two words don't go together, so I looked with closer interest. Beside the blind skier was another man wearing an orange vest with just one word: *Guide.*

We all reached the top, and Natalie and I stayed a few moments to see how they would do this. The blind skier got set, and the guide got behind him and hooked ropes to either side of the blind man's vest. The guide held the ropes as they took off down the slope and kept calling just two words, over and over: "Right. Left. Right. Left."

I watched them off and on throughout the day. The blind man skied just as fast as I did, yet I could see where I was going. The two of them kept going up and down all the slopes and having a wonderful time. I thought about the courage it took for this blind man to step onto the slopes, knowing that just ahead were trees lining the sides of the runs and crazy people skiing all around him. I know. I was one of them. There were little moguls all the way down the slope that you could hit and fall over. But the blind man put on his skis and put his absolute trust in a man he could not see to guide him through all the obstacles.

That is exactly what Jesus wants us to do. That is the kind of commitment Jesus was asking for that day from Peter, Andrew, James, and John as He called them to follow Him and become fishers of men. And they did it. They dropped everything and followed with absolute trust and courage, knowing that their guide would not let them hit the trees.

The question we need to face is simple: What do you and I need to drop? What is it today that you are holding on to, not willing to give up because it feels safe? That load of fish must have called powerfully to those fishermen. Man, they could have taken all those fish and gone to the merchants and sold the catch. They could have made a mint, put away a little nest egg, maybe bought bigger boats, invested in some security. They felt safe in the routines of the fishing life. It was all they had ever known. They could have gone out the next day onto the lake and caught fish and done that day after day, just as they had been doing. They might have seen that as a smooth way of life. But they forsook all and followed Jesus. They dropped the nets.

What do you need to drop? We all have something that we cling to. It may simply be sin. You may feel so caught up in sin that you can't get free. You are addicted, and you don't know how to walk away. Your net might be in a bottle or syringe. It might be on a website or in a magazine. You are holding on to it, or perhaps more truly it is holding on to you.

Maybe the net that entangles you is a bad relationship. You have made all the mistakes in your marriage or relationship, and you are butting heads every day with your partner. But you don't know what to do so you just carry on. That is a net you could be holding on to. I'm not saying that you should walk away from the marriage. I am saying, get help. Drop the nets of your problems and let Jesus bring you through in victory.

Maybe you are caught up in money problems. Perhaps you are in a secure position with a job that is providing everything you want, but you find money has a grip on you. You must have the right stuff, and this kind of house, and that kind of car, and certain clothes and a designer purse to go with them. Or quite possibly your money problems take the form of worry over never having enough, and you live in fear of the bottom dropping out of your personal economy. Money problems are nets that can hold on to you.

I repeat the question: What do you need to drop? Matthew couldn't have made a difference in the world if he had gone back to the tax collector's table the next day. The same could be said of Peter had he simply gone back to fishing. Jesus had called them to something else. They only became world-changers when they dropped the stuff that had a hold on them. Their response to Jesus' call was to forsake everything and follow Him. What will be your response?

To start, you need to put your trust in Jesus as Savior, dropping whatever it is you are holding on to, and just start following wherever He decides to lead you. In this, you will begin an adventure that includes forgiveness, purpose, fulfillment, and rest for your soul. As you are transformed, your part in changing the world will involve living a life that matters, being a small light in your corner of the world. In the chapters ahead we will see how that plays out.

Questions for Individual Reflection
or Small Group Discussion

1. In what senses are you an *ordinary* person? Are there any senses in which you are not?
2. Why do you think Jesus mostly chose common people to follow Him?
3. Take a look at some of Jesus' twelve disciples mentioned in this chapter. Which disciple are you perhaps most like and why?
4. When Jesus asks a person to follow Him, what kind of commitment is He asking for?
5. How can God take your life and make it count for eternity?

4

THE OFFER: SUPREME
HAPPINESS

Not many of us will ever do what Jim and Maud Watt did back in 1918. Jim worked for the Hudson's Bay Company, a name that has found its place in history books as the force that opened the fur trade in the Canadian wilds over a span of several hundred years. Jim and his young wife, Maud, had built Fort Chimo on the Labrador coast, an outpost reached only by ship. Their job was to trade with the Indians and Eskimos, largely nomadic people who ranged over that frozen territory. The native people traded furs for food and supplies.

The Watts' eyes had grown dim that year as they continued their watch from shore for the supply ship. That annual ship was their lifeline to the outside, bringing staples for them and the post. But the season was over, and no ship was in sight. They suspected that their ship had either run into trouble or been diverted to the war effort in Europe, and by October they knew no relief ship could be counted on for at least another year. A company post can't stay in business without trade goods, and it was uncertain how long the little settlement could ward off starvation.[1]

Jim knew that if supplies couldn't be sent by ship, they needed to find a way to bring them in overland. His companions wondered at his sanity. Overland meant crossing Ungava Peninsula, a vast expanse of ice, tundra, and bare rock, in temperatures that hovered around thirty to fifty degrees below zero. No Eskimos or Indians had ever crossed the entire Ungava Peninsula, and several white men had died trying.

But they had to go. Jim plotted a course of about eight hundred miles north to south, planning to haul the trek supplies on just one sled. A few Indian guides and Maud would go, too, adding her expertise in Indian culture. Ungava is pretty much a giant plateau ironed over by an ice sheet. Smack in the middle is a dividing ridge called the Height of Land. From there rocky plains incline downward to every compass point with complex rivers flowing north, east, south, and west. More than half the surface is under water, so the Watts started in winter to take advantage of the ice cover for using a sled. They hoped that by the time they reached the Height of Land, the ice would have broken in the southern watershed, and they could go on by canoe.

The trip was unimaginably difficult. To get to the Height of Land, Jim needed to haul a dogsled—by himself—for more than a month, about four hundred miles through trackless wilderness. A sickness among the dogs was the reason for pulling the sled by manpower. You can imagine the hardships they endured in that trek, including hunger, snow blindness, frostbite, and exhaustion.

But they succeeded! Exactly one month after leaving Fort Chimo, they reached the Height of Land. The setting sun flooded the white land with redness and a stark beauty. Jim and Maud felt an elation that could find no words.

While it wasn't exactly all downhill from there, and many trials were yet to be faced, from the Height of Land the Watts renewed their hope. In another month they reached civilization and became the first people ever known to cross Ungava Peninsula. The overland route they established opened the North and became the basis for a future railway, mining explorations, and air bases.

It is that scene at the Height of Land I want us to consider—the elation, the hope, the sense of achievement—while behind is hardship and before is the unknown. That high place, even in the midst of trouble, seems to be a fitting symbol of the place we all aspire to, the height of happiness.

As we examine a particular scene from Jesus' 1,000-day ministry, we will see that He talked about something He called heightened happiness. It is something we all want. We want it so badly that we can taste it, so badly that we try all kinds of schemes to get to this place. Maybe you have been willing to put in huge efforts because you think a certain path will lead to the height of happiness. You might be willing to work hard, play hard, dream hard. Or perhaps you have been willing sometimes even to manipulate, cheat, and steal to reach your personal concept of the height of happiness.

How is that working for you so far? Maybe when you pause and think about it, you realize you would like to have been there that day when Jesus gathered some people around Him on a mountainside and offered them the secret.

THE SECRET OF TRUE HAPPINESS

In the last chapter, we watched Jesus move around the shore of the Sea of Galilee and call some ordinary people to follow Him. Matthew's gospel tells us that He went throughout the area, teaching and healing, and news about Him spread even beyond the Galilee region. People in need began seeking Him out, and crowds began to follow Him everywhere—people in pain, people in sin, people oppressed by demons, people in need of happiness, people with all kinds of needs. And He met those needs.

His fame spread. People began to see folks who once were lame and now could walk. People who had been demon-possessed were now free and acting normally. Sick people had been made well. The crowds came to check Him out. They wanted to see what in the world was going on, and they flooded after Him. But whether they knew it or not, they were beyond being simply curious. Every one of them was a person in need.

Matthew tells us Jesus taught in their synagogues. On a trip to the land of Israel, I visited Capernaum near the Sea of Galilee at the ruins of a synagogue from Jesus' day. You can walk right into the excavated ruins. Archaeologists have dug down seven or eight feet to reveal layers of stones that had been built upon each other, and later the buildings had crumbled. They have uncovered the bottom, and you can see the actual stone floor of this synagogue, where Jesus taught two thousand years ago. The story comes alive when you visit the place.

I can imagine how that Capernaum synagogue overflowed with people coming to see what Jesus would do. They probably had to throw open the doors of the synagogue so people who couldn't squeeze in could just get a glimpse of Him and hear a little of what He was saying. The place was packed. Talk about a successful ministry. But Jesus wanted to get away from the crowds and walk out through the gates of Capernaum and up into the Galilee hills as Matthew 5:1 tells us.

You can follow His route today. Just above Capernaum on a hillside, you will find the Church of the Beatitudes, built in 1938 upon the ruins of a Byzantine church from the fourth century. Tradition says Jesus came to this spot when He left the synagogue that day and delivered the Sermon on the Mount. There is a beautiful view, down over the rolling slopes to the Galilee farming region, the Sea of Galilee, and the little towns where people lived.

Jesus gathered His disciples around, and with all the beauty of that scene in view, He shared a story of a place that is far more beautiful and told of a kind of happiness that is beyond any they could find in the routine of their lives.

Here is what He told them:

> "Blessed are the poor in spirit,
>   For theirs is the kingdom of heaven.
> Blessed are those who mourn,
>   For they shall be comforted.
> Blessed are the meek,
>   For they shall inherit the earth.
> Blessed are those who hunger and thirst for righteousness,
>   For they shall be filled.
> Blessed are the merciful,
>   For they shall obtain mercy.
> Blessed are the pure in heart,
>   For they shall see God.

Blessed are the peacemakers,
  For they shall be called sons of God.
Blessed are those who are persecuted for righteousness' sake,
  For theirs is the kingdom of heaven.

"Blessed are you when they revile and persecute you, and say all kinds of evil against you falsely for My sake. Rejoice and be exceedingly glad, for great is your reward in heaven, for so they persecuted the prophets who were before you." (Matt. 5:3–12)

You are probably familiar with those words. These statements are called the Beatitudes, a word that simply means "heightened happiness" or "supreme blessedness." Jesus was saying, "Look, here is your Height of Land. Although there may be trouble all around you, in your past and even in your future, you can know true happiness. Your spirit can live in this blessed place." When Jesus gathered people around Him that day, He knew each one desired to live in happiness, just as we do.

You probably noticed He began every statement with the word *blessed*. In the Greek language it is the word *makarios*, which literally means "divinely given contentment and peace." If that's what you want—heightened happiness, divinely given contentment and peace, joy with an added dimension, life with abundance—here's what you do, according to Jesus. He gave them a checklist for how to live in this blessed place.

GOING OVER THE HAPPINESS CHECKLIST

Look at the first item Jesus told them to check: "Blessed are the poor in spirit." When we see the word *poor*, we tend to think of finances. We may think we fall into that category if we can't afford to pay our mortgage or rent or car payment. Maybe we feel poor if we can't go buy a new computer or some technological gadget. Or if we can't buy our kids the things they clamor for or if we can't dress in the latest style. Maybe *poor* to us means not being able to take a vacation. Or it could be more serious, such as the grocery money that is not going to stretch to the next paycheck. But none of those things form the context for Jesus' words.

The word *poor* that Jesus used is the Greek word *ptokos*. The definition is "totally destitute, totally impoverished." Jesus is saying that we are blessed when we realize we don't have anything at all without Him. We are completely impoverished and lack everything if we don't have Him. Without His provision, we don't have any means to take care of our physical needs. Without Him, we have no emotional resources. Without Him, we are depleted of mental resources and our educational qualifications mean nothing. Without Him, when it comes to spiritual things, we are dead broke. Total dependence on God is the first item on the checklist for heightened happiness. How are you doing in that area? If you are poor in spirit, you realize that you are totally destitute, but the kingdom of heaven is yours. That is, you gain everything when you realize you have nothing.

Matthew 5:4 says, "Blessed are those who mourn." We may think of mourning in the context of funerals and losing someone we love. The definition of this word goes right along with that. *Mourn* is the Greek word *pentheo* and means "strong, heavy weeping or lamenting." Have you had times when tears literally flow down your cheeks, you feel utterly brokenhearted, and you can't go on? That is this kind of mourning. It seems strange that Jesus would say we are actually blessed, or in "heightened happiness," when we are mourning as heavily as this. But we need to understand that Jesus used this same word when He mourned over the sins of the people of Jerusalem. And so here in Matthew 5, He was saying that we are blessed, not when we are sad about a loss in our lives, but when we are so broken over sin that we actually mourn over it. He was telling us that one key to heightened happiness is to recognize sin in our lives and mourn over it.

You see, it is possible to get so deep into sin that it doesn't bother us much anymore. Sometimes sin seems as though it is not such a big deal. It no longer jumps out and grabs us as to how serious it is. You may remember watching TV or a movie as a child and hearing a cuss word. Remember what we did? Probably, we all winced. We couldn't believe that would actually be allowed on television. We hoped that our parents in the next room didn't hear it. But you know what happens? The more we hear that kind of thing, the more we get desensitized, and pretty soon we are not wincing at all. Sometimes we don't even notice. It is possible to move further and further into a sinful life until sin no longer bothers us. We are not just hearing it; we are doing it. We are no longer broken over sin, no longer weeping over sin, even our own sin, because it just doesn't seem like such a big deal.

Jesus says those who actually mourn over sin are blessed and they will be comforted. It brings to mind the wonderful truth of 1 John 1:9 that tells us if we confess our sins He is faithful and just, according to His character, and will forgive and cleanse us. That sounds a lot like, "Blessed are those who mourn for they shall be comforted." We are blessed when we are bothered by sin and repent because those sins will be replaced by divinely given contentment. The second item on our checklist for heightened happiness is being sensitive to sin in our lives and around us.

Matthew 5:5 says, "Blessed are the meek." Let's be clear that being meek doesn't mean being mealy-mouthed or weak. It's not about going around being proud of your excessive humility. It has to do with not grasping for your own rights. That word *meek* in the original language is *praus*. It means "power under control, power in submission to God." We don't like to give up control. We like to keep control over every element of our lives. We want an absolute handle on everything we do, every place we go, everything we see. Jesus was telling us to give over the control of all that to Him.

Jesus Himself modeled this perfectly. Do you remember the incident in the Garden of Gethsemane where Judas betrays Him? Soldiers grabbed Jesus and then led Him off to be beaten and battered, made fun of and mocked, and taken to Calvary. But looking ahead to all of this from Gethsemane, Jesus made this important statement to His Father: "Not as I will, but as You will" (Matt. 26:39). He also said that He could have called ten thousand angels to come and help Him resist. But God the Son modeled for us the submission of control to God the Father.

Our checklist question is, "Am I constantly focusing on and seeking God's will for my life?"

The next beatitude Jesus gives us is Matthew 5:6: "Blessed are those who hunger and thirst for righteousness." This is about those who have a deep desire to get to know God, to study His Word, to learn more deeply who He really is and what He has to say to us.

One evening our family was driving back from Wintergreen, the ski hill. We had gone skiing again, and I broke no bones, which is really cool. As we drove for that hour or so, we were reading the Bible. Jessica started reading in Matthew 28, and then Nicholas and Natalie read Mark 1, and Jonathan read Mark 2, just enjoying together the wisdom of God's Word. Whether it is formal or informal times, getting into God's Word is a way of expressing our hunger and thirst for righteousness.

God says when we do that, we will be filled. That word *filled* is the Greek word *chortadzo*, and it literally means "to fill, to satisfy with food, to fatten." In our day we would say it means to be utterly stuffed.

When I was in high school, family friends Ed and Donna Hindson took me to a Japanese steak house in Roanoke. I had never been to any place like that before because I hated both seafood and rice, but they assured me I would love it. They promised me that if I really didn't like it they would take me to McDonald's afterward. So I was in.

The servers cooked the shrimp in front of us and put it on our plates and threw the tails all over the room. And I was thinking, *I'm not going to eat that stuff.* But Donna said, "Try it. You will love it." So I picked up my fork because she was my elder and I'd been raised to respect my elders. I stabbed the fork into the shrimp, dipped it in the sauce, and ate it—and it was incredible. I ate it all and sent for another order. Then I ordered steak and chicken. They cooked that in front of us, too, and did the volcanoes and all and piled it on my plate along with a heap of rice. I said, "I hate rice. I'm not going to eat rice." But Donna said, "Seriously, just try the rice." So I took a bit of rice and dipped it in the ginger sauce. It was unbelievable. I ate all of it!

Now many years later rarely does a week go by that we don't get Japanese food. I eat it all, and you know what happens every time you eat a lot of rice. It grows inside you. It's like having your own little rice paddy going on in there. It expands, and soon you feel ready to explode. You feel absolutely stuffed.

Jesus is saying those who hunger and thirst for righteousness will be filled, utterly stuffed with the blessings of God. We will be full to overflowing with God's goodness, and it will feel wonderful. Our checklist principle is that we need to be hungry to get to know God better every day.

The passage goes on in Matthew 5:7 to say, "Blessed are the merciful." Jesus was saying that life is way too short to hold grudges. Maybe someone has done something to upset you and, yes, it really hurt and was really wrong. It might be a coworker or even your spouse. You can't get it out of your mind or stop holding on to the pain it caused you. But Jesus is saying that if you act in a merciful way, meaning you always want the other person to win, you will experience heightened happiness. You should be willing to give, to seek to build relationships, to make sure everything is good between you and the other person. It's about forgiveness. When you extend mercy to someone, you, too, will obtain mercy. Maybe not from that person then and there, but your reserve tank of mercy will be filled up. Can you imagine what your relationships would be like if you were always willing to forgive at the drop of a hat? Our checklist principle is to examine ourselves to see that we are not so much seeking to win as we are wanting others to be winners.

THE CHECKLIST CONTINUES

Matthew 5:8 says, "Blessed are the pure in heart, for they shall see God." Those who are pure in heart have selfless motives and seek to ensure doing the right thing. Jesus said if that is our focus, if that is who we are, we will see God. The Greek word for *see* is the word *optanomai*. It simply means "see." It's hard to elaborate on that definition. The word *optanomai* is the root of our English word *optimal*. So Jesus was saying that the pure in heart, those who have selfless motives will have an optimal view of God. You get an unobstructed view of who God is; there is nothing to distract you or get in your way. Your view of His goodness and greatness is not blocked by sin or selfishness. On the checklist, ask yourself: Are my motives pure? Am I living a life that is pure in heart with no cheating, lying, or deceiving?

Matthew 5:9 says, "Blessed are the peacemakers." When we think of peacemakers, it may come to mind that a big part of a parent's job is to try to keep peace between kids in the family. But that is not what Jesus was talking about here. He is referring to people who desperately need to make peace with God. In other words, if you are helping people reach that place, you are blessed. The checklist principle is to ask yourself if you are passionate about reaching people with the gospel of Jesus Christ so they can know peace with God. If so, you are in a state of heightened happiness.

Matthew 5:10–11 says, "Blessed are those who are persecuted for righteousness' sake. . . . Blessed are you when they revile and persecute you, and say all kinds of evil against you falsely for My sake." Jesus added that we should be glad when that happens, for the prophets who came before us were also persecuted.

Jesus never promised us that living His way would be easy. A lifestyle that fits the kingdom principles is no bed of roses. He told us clearly there would be tough days and there would be people who come after us and attack us for what we believe and what we stand for.

You may have heard that Chick-fil-A took some heat from various groups because of the company's position not to open its restaurants on Sundays. Attackers have tried to get cities to sever contracts with Chick-fil-A and get the restaurants thrown off college campuses. Truett Cathy started Chick-fil-A in the early sixtes, and his son, Dan Cathy, leads the still privately held and family-owned restaurant business today. They answered the critics in the news media saying, in effect, that they were not going to throw their Christian beliefs out the window. Here's what I have to say about that: eat more chicken!

The promise is that you will be attacked for your faith; you will be reviled and persecuted. But you can rejoice when it happens because your reward will be huge. Just as Jesus took the crowd up to the mountainside by Galilee that day, He takes us up from this world system full of evil. He moves us to a place of divinely given contentment, of heightened happiness. We live in a place that this world can't touch. Our checklist principle is to resolve that whatever we face, we are committed not to quit.

LIVING BY THE PRINCIPLES THAT PRODUCE HAPPINESS

Review the checklist for heightened happiness as you honestly review your life. Ask yourself these questions:

1. Am I depending on God for everything?
2. Am I sensitive to sin in my life and in this world?
3. Am I constantly focused on God's will for my life?
4. Am I hungry to get to know God better every day?
5. Am I living a life that's selfless, wanting everyone to win?
6. Am I living with pure motives in my heart?
7. Am I passionate to recruit others to God and to living His way?
8. Am I committed that no matter how hard it gets, I will never quit?

Ask forgiveness of God in the areas where your life falls down. Give control to your Savior. Resolve to grow in the principles where you need improvement. The result of living this way is really no secret at all; it's simply happiness.

QUESTIONS FOR INDIVIDUAL REFLECTION
OR SMALL GROUP DISCUSSION

1. What things make you most happy and why?
2. Jesus said, "Blessed are the poor in spirit." By this, He meant that when it comes to spiritual things, we are dead broke. How have you seen this to be true in your own life?
3. Have you ever been so disturbed by sin that you actually mourn over it? Jesus tells us that one key to heightened happiness is to recognize sin in our lives and mourn over it. How have you seen this to be true (or not) in your own life?
4. What does it look like to be truly meek, in other words, to give control of all aspects of your life to Jesus?
5. Which of the Beatitudes do you tend to most closely associate with and why?

5

Smooth Sailing
versus Calmed Storm

Once, a group of men longed to be pirates.

In their mind's eye was a picture of grand adventure. They longed to get out on the high seas. To them, the whole idea of pirating was all about fun and reward. They decided that the next time they heard that a certain famous pirate was in port, they would join his ship, sail the seven seas with him, and search for glory and gold.

One day this group of men spotted the renowned old pirate pulling in to dock his boat. They ran up to his pirate ship and called out, "Aye, Captain, we want to join your crew. Bid us aboard."

After a moment they heard a raspy, deep voice over the hull saying, "So you want to be pirates, eh?"

They weren't yet able to see him over the side of the ship, but called out, "Aye, Captain, we want to be part of your crew."

Suddenly they heard a strange sound: *step, thump, step, thump, step, thump.* Coming into view was an old, dirty, scarred pirate with a weather-beaten hat and a thick leather jacket frayed at the edges. He had an unkempt beard and a stump for a leg, a hook for a hand, and an eye patch.

They began talking all at once: "Aye, Captain, we want to follow you. Yes-siree. We want to join up."

He held up his hook for a hand to silence the group and drawled, "So you want to be pirates, huh? It ain't easy, boys."

One guy in the crowd looked over the old pirate more closely and thought, *Hmm. Maybe he's telling the truth.* He looked the old captain in the eye and asked, "Captain, what happened to your leg?"

The veteran pirate answered, "Well, I was commandeering an enemy ship. Fell overboard and a twenty-eight-foot shark chewed off my foot. Leg turned all gangrene, and they had to cut it off at the knee. Pirating ain't easy, boys. That's how I got my stump of a leg."

One of the group dared to ask another question: "Captain, sir, I have to ask, how did you get your hook?"

The old pirate said, "Aye, there was mutiny, my boy, and I was in a duel, and the other guy cut off my hand with his sword. So I got me this hook. Pirating ain't easy, I tell ya."

Now the whole crowd of wannabe pirates was rethinking the idea. Some stepped back. This didn't sound much like the glorious adventure they had envisioned. The first man who dared to speak out had one more burning question: "Captain, I've got to know, what happened to your eye?"

The captain fixed him with his one good eye, swatted at a fly near his face, and said, "Aye, it happened the first day with me hook."

Apart from the humor the story shows us a picture of an experienced insider presenting a way of life as it really is—in this case, a life characterized by hardship. That is exactly the point Jesus made with His wannabe followers: the adventure of the Christian life is not a bed of roses, not easy street.

Maybe you have learned that already. You started out on this adventure with Jesus, and you are finding it is definitely not smooth sailing. Sometimes you feel like retreating. Often you feel unsure that you will even survive what life throws at you. You doubt that you have what it takes to be a committed follower of Jesus. Maybe you haven't decided to follow Jesus yet, and you are trying to take a clear-eyed look at what it might actually be like. You have arrived at a crossroads.

It's a great question for anyone to ask: What does it mean to truly follow Jesus?

REACHING A PIVOT POINT WITH JESUS

In the last chapter we watched Jesus gather His followers up on a mountain and give them special teaching about happiness; in fact, we watched Him offer the secrets to heightened happiness. It turns out that happiness is not the whole story. Jesus' teaching on the Beatitudes launched Him into a whole body of teaching known as the Sermon on the Mount, found in Matthew 5–7, which describes what it is like to live His way. Along with His teaching, Jesus continued to do miracles. Great masses of people began following Him, crowds upon crowds.

But Jesus was not into the numbers game. He did not depend on huge crowds for success, and He did not glory in His impressive following. He was more concerned that each follower came after Him for the right reasons, and that each one truly understood what he was getting into.

When we see Jesus at this point in His 1,000-day ministry, we see Him in the midst of hundreds and sometimes thousands of people. These masses traveled with Him and followed after Him from all the regions of Galilee, Judea, Decapolis, Idumea, and all the other regions. But we find that Jesus constantly split the crowds in half.

For instance, one time He fed five thousand men plus women and children—probably at least fifteen thousand people—with some fish and bread that didn't exist before. He did it simply by a creative miracle, and people recognized that and were awed. They kept on following Him and asked if they could have more food to eat, if they could see more of the magic show.

The story in John 6 recounts how Jesus taught them about a far more important kind of bread—Himself. He encouraged them to believe in Him as the Bread of Life. This deep-core belief would fully and eternally satisfy them, not just give temporary satisfaction as did the loaves on the hillside. He wanted them to consume every single truth about Him. He did not want them to follow simply to see miracles or just because He was the flavor of the month. He wanted them to follow because they fully believed, because they understood who He was and what He had come to do.

But they as much as those in the sixth chapter of John said, "Forget it." They wanted to keep talking about their stomachs. They focused on the here and now and on their immediate appetites. The sad thing that happens is that many of His so-called followers, then and now, turn away when they realize it involves a full commitment and it's not all fun and games.

The pivotal point in our relationship with Christ is when we begin to follow Him for the right reasons, when we determine to keep going even when we see it won't be easy. We may be weather-beaten, ship-wrecked, exhausted, and dragged through all kinds of hardships, but we will follow Him anyway because we know who He is. We never lose sight of the fact that Jesus is 100 percent God and 100 percent human at the same time, and He is worth following, come what may.

Maybe you are not quite there yet. Perhaps you came to God because you heard it was about love and joy and provision and answers to prayer, and who wouldn't want that? Or you might be considering coming to God because someone has painted for you a rosy picture of the Christian life that sounds good. Maybe you are following from a long way back because you have certain fears about what will happen if you get too close up behind Jesus. For those who are not quite there yet, a telling story is found in Matthew 8.

FOLLOWING JESUS FOR THE RIGHT REASONS

Soon after He preached the Sermon on the Mount, Jesus left the multitudes and had a one-on-one conversation with a man who didn't quite understand the weight of following Christ. The man was in love with the idea of jumping on board with Jesus' nice-sounding teachings. Apparently following Jesus appealed to him as a life of ease and a way to make things better. He had a few things to learn.

Jesus was just about to get into a boat and cross to the other side of the lake when this man grabbed Him by the arm and boldly declared, "Teacher, I will follow You wherever You go" (Matt. 8:19).

Good statement, right? Sounds as though he was willing to follow anywhere, anytime. Except that Jesus could see into the man's heart, just as He can see into yours and mine. He saw that something was amiss.

It's important to notice that the man was a scribe, a teacher of the law. Up to this point in Jesus' ministry, scribes had never been sympathetic to Him. In fact, the scribes were some of the biggest sources of hostility. They constantly interrupted His teaching and tried to debate Him and incite arguments. They hogged His time and pushed away people who sincerely wanted to learn. They tried to trap Him in embarrassing statements or even illegal slip-ups.

In Luke's account of Jesus' 1,000-day ministry, Jesus acted in a way that theologians have called the Great Reversal. It means He took people of lowly status and put them into crucial roles in His parables and teachings. He built lessons and illustrations around shepherds, children, beggars, and abused women. You almost never find a story of Jesus that is about a wealthy or powerful person. The scribes did not like this reversal. They would sometimes drag a sinful person right into the middle of one of Jesus' teaching sessions to try to embarrass him or her, such as the adulterous woman whose story is told in John 8. They mocked what to them seemed like a ridiculous message of mercy. They would say to Him, "We know the law. What are You going to do with this sinful person? Here is this unclean, unworthy person who wants to be a follower. Are You gonna have her on Your side?"

That's the kind of thing the scribes commonly did. And it is one of these scribes who came to Jesus in Matthew 8 and declared he would follow Jesus anywhere. Jesus looked into his heart, which is no problem for Him to do, and saw that this was one of the guys who loved the fanfare, the fame, the pomp, and the preferred seating. Jesus told the scribe that when he could solve his heart problem, he would be able to become a true follower.

Here is how Jesus put it: "Foxes have holes and birds of the air have nests, but the Son of Man has nowhere to lay His head" (Matt. 8:20). Jesus knew the man had an issue with material possessions; he knew that the scribe was not ready to give up all that he had. His motives were all wrong. The scribe was probably thinking there was some material gain to be had in following Jesus; after all, Jesus was the one who had multiplied the loaves and fish. What could He do with bank accounts?

I don't know if the scribe realized it, but all the way through the 1,000 days of Jesus' intensive ministry, He hardly ever had anywhere to lay His head. Artists often picture Him at His birth as this glorious baby in a glowing aura, but actually when He touched down on planet Earth, He didn't even have a room in the inn. He had to sleep in an animal's feeding trough in a stable. A stable was just an attachment to a house or a dugout cave where shepherds could put their animals for the night. It was a smelly, dirty place, no doubt, and some hay gathered from the ground had probably been thrown into the manger with a semi-clean blanket tossed over it. That was where God the Son laid His head when He first entered the world. As an adult out ministering with His disciples, Jesus probably often said something like, "Come on, let's go to the hillside and take our rest. Pick the best rock you can find, boys."

Even when He died, Jesus had no place to lay His head. There is a tomb outside Jerusalem today that may have been the very one where Jesus' body was laid. Certainly it is similar to the one His body was placed in. This particular tomb reflects wealth, with several spacious levels, and must have been quite an investment. But it belonged to Joseph of Arimathea. Yes, it was one of the bigger tombs, but it was a borrowed tomb. Even at His death Jesus had nowhere of His own to lay His head. Why is it that people like the scribe or maybe like you and me tend to feel entitled? Why do we expect Him to lavish us with blessings and give us a prosperous life as if we deserve it? Sadly, there is no record that the scribe ever became a follower of Jesus with pure motives, willing to drop everything and simply follow Jesus because of who He is.

Following Jesus into the Storm

What happened next was a situation with which I am sure we can identify. We can easily feel right in the middle of this. Matthew records the well-known story of Jesus and His disciples caught in the storm. This set of conditions sounds very familiar. Not one of us gets through life without some storms.

You may be ready to acknowledge that the Christian life is not a bed of roses, and you accept that. You are okay with it because you have a pretty full load of blessings, you have managed to sidestep the biggest disasters, and you have great friendships with other followers of Jesus who help you through the rough patches. You understand that Jesus said it could get hard, and you know there is an element of taking up your cross to follow Him. But honestly, you never thought it would get this bad. You may feel blindsided by a set of conditions that you were never prepared for, never imagined in your wildest moments. It has left you reeling.

We need to pay attention to what happened next in the story. Jesus walked away from that man, the scribe who wasn't ready to follow Him wholly. He climbed into the boat that His disciples had waiting, and they headed out onto the Sea of Galilee.

Matthew 8:24 says, "And suddenly a great tempest arose on the sea, so that the boat was covered with the waves." This was no tiny squall. The little Sea of Galilee is a place that typically develops storms very quickly. There are mountains all around it. When a strong wind whips through, the terrain forms a kind of funnel for the wind, and these waters can get really stirred up. When you are out there and start seeing storm clouds coming, you need to head for shore immediately. It's not a large lake, only about thirteen miles long by eight miles wide. But the lightning can flash and the thunder crash and the ripples turn to chop, and the chop becomes waves and swells and rollers so that even experienced fishermen are scared to death. Those who live around the Sea of Galilee will tell you that some of the storms that hit there can be the scariest you can experience.

The words used in verse 24, *great tempest*, are taken from one Greek word *seismos*. *Seismos* is used fourteen times in the New Testament, but only this once does it speak of a storm. For the other thirteen times the word is reserved for cataclysmic earthquakes. But apparently this storm was so bad that Matthew could best describe it with the word usually used for calamitous earthquakes. This was the worst of the worst. Can you imagine being out there in that? You are tossing wildly, you can't control anything with your puny oars, you can't hear each other yell, the waves swamp the boat, and you are sure the next one will finish you.

Where was Jesus in all this? He was in the bow of the boat asleep. You see, Jesus is not only fully God but fully human. Often during His earthly life He got tired and hungry because He lived in a human body just like we do. It is no surprise to find Him here catching a nap.

Matthew 8:25 says, "Then His disciples came to Him and awoke Him, saying, 'Lord, save us! We are perishing!'" They shook His shoulder and yelled into His face. Some translations say, "Don't you care that we are perishing?" I guess it felt to them, when He simply went on sleeping through all this, as though He didn't even care.

Watch what happened next. Perhaps He yawned and stretched and wiped the sleep out of His eyes. Then He chided them a little, asking why they were so fearful and where their faith had gone. But this was much more than a little sermon. Next He stood up and did an absolutely amazing thing: "He arose and rebuked the winds and the sea, and there was a great calm. So the men marveled, saying, 'Who can this be, that even the winds and the sea obey Him?'" (Matt. 8:26–27). Mark tells us in his gospel the exact words Jesus spoke to the sea. Catch this: "He arose and rebuked the wind, and said to the sea, 'Peace, be still!' And the wind ceased and there was a great calm" (Mark 4:39).

Siopao is the Greek word used here for *peace*. *Be still* is a translation of the Greek word *phimoo*, and it is an action word, meaning "to muzzle." Jesus was actually saying, "Hush, hush, shh-h, shh-h," similar to what we would say to a child who is complaining or a baby who just can't calm down. He shushed the storm. He imposed a gag order on this powerful phenomenon of nature.

As soon as His words hit, the storm stopped. The wind and waves didn't ease gradually, as with a naturally subsiding storm. The men looked around at an instantly glassy, calm surface. They must have sat there with their mouths hanging open.

Lessons in the Aftermath
of the Storm

After the disciples' faithless response Jesus rebuked them in Matthew 8:26: "But He said to them, 'Why are you fearful, O you of little faith?' Then He arose and rebuked the winds and the sea, and there was a great calm." Notice that besides a big rebuke for the storm, Jesus had a smaller rebuke for the disciples. He fully understood their fears; He doesn't fault us for being human and weak. But He rebuked them, and He rebukes us when we forget in the midst of our fears to put our faith in Him. Our part is always to turn to the One who is utterly calm in the middle of our storms, the One who can take all our troubled waters and calm them. We should know by now that this is how He works, and we simply should trust Him continually.

We live in a kind of tension of truth. It brings to mind the wonderful truth of Philippians 3:10. Jesus calls us to take up our cross and promises that we will have trouble and persecution. On the other hand He promises us an abundant life with heightened happiness and that He Himself will calm our storms. These words written by Paul to the believers in the town of Philippi refer to the same tension of truth.

"That I may know Him and the power of His resurrection, and the fellowship of His sufferings, being conformed to His death" (Phil. 3:10). Paul was saying he wanted to know God experientially, up close and personal. That partly involves grasping the power and victory of Jesus' resurrection; but Paul also understood that it involves joining him in suffering and death-like experiences.

Jesus calls us today to the experience of cross-bearing, to die to our self-focus and in a small way to identify with what He did for us. He calls us to a ministry of suffering over sin as He did. No, we can't suffer for sin in an atoning way, in a way that pays for it even a little bit, as He did. But we can grieve over it. And it may mean being persecuted or enduring slander or being spoken of falsely. Believers of old and in other cultures have been stoned and beaten and bruised, and some have died for the cause of Christ. We may face that kind of severe storm. He calls on us to let our hearts grieve over sin and to have a constant burden for friends and loved ones to find the Lord. This does not describe an easy road or smooth sailing on a calm lake. But He also calls on us to trust Him to calm the storms.

BRINGING OUR STORMS TO HIM

The question today is, "What storm do you need Jesus to calm?"

You may be going through some terrible turmoil in your life, perhaps triggered by your own sin or stupidity or perhaps through no fault of your own. You may have been faithful to Him but have a divided family. Those closest to you at home or at work or in your neighborhood might be slandering you, bringing lawsuits against you, dragging your name in the mud. Perhaps you are in a storm of financial problems that hit with a fury and suddenness you never expected and were not prepared for. Maybe you are a victim of bullying, or your storm is about health or relationships. It could be a storm of depression or a battering of suicidal thoughts. Maybe a torrent is brewing in your heart, unseen by everyone, because you wrestle with God about some issue. You are angry at Him or resisting Him. Whatever your storm is, you know you can't navigate these waters by yourself.

The answer is so simple that it is easy to miss. Do you remember what the disciples did that day in the boat? They simply called on Jesus. They gave Him their helplessness and their doubts, and He did the rest. He calmed the storm. He is bigger than any of our storms, He is never flustered by them, and He absolutely has enough power to handle them.

Jesus still calms storms today. That doesn't necessarily mean He makes all your troubles go away. It is not always the storms of circumstance that He calms; sometimes it is the storms within your heart. He doesn't always make the physical waves flatline, but He always offers perfect calm to ride through them. As for the circumstances, He will either still those waves or ride them out with you. You will never be left alone at the mercy of any storm. He could, of course, wrap you inside a plastic bubble and prevent any storms from ever coming into your life. But sometimes He allows a storm to break so that you may learn important lessons and be brought closer to Him. Even obedience on your part may lead you directly into the path of a storm. But His resources are always enough. He promises a limitless supply of strength, equal to your needs.

Bird-watchers have observed that as a storm approaches most birds seek shelter. They flit away to hide in their nests or in the trees or the little rocky caves in the cleft of a rock-face. But the eagle is an exception. The eagle faces the storm, spreads its wings, and allows it to carry him to the heights. In the high places above the storm's fury, the eagle is able to ride it out in safety. That's Jesus' invitation to you. To fly through the storm like an eagle. The view from the heights is fantastic.

Questions for Individual Reflection or Small Group Discussion

1. If someone said to you, "Following Jesus makes your life better," how would you respond to that? Do you think it's always true all the time, partially true some of the time, or not true at all? Or perhaps it matters how a person defines "better." Discuss.

2. When Jesus describes Himself as "the bread of life," He means that when people commune with Him they'll be fully and eternally satisfied, not just temporarily satisfied as with eating regular food. How have you seen Jesus to be "the bread of life"? What might this mean, or not mean?

3. Jesus calms the storms in our lives. What storm do you need Jesus to calm in your life?

4. What does it mean to identify with Jesus' work, including His suffering?

5. Why is it so important that people understand what Jesus truly offers—and doesn't offer? What can happen when people think Jesus offers them things He never promised? What can happen when people truly grasp what He offers them?

6

THE WAY OF
RADICAL LOVE

What does it mean to truly love?

The last words of Sydney Carton answer this question and burn into your memory, even though he was a fictional character. In Charles Dickens's classic book *A Tale of Two Cities*, Sydney Carton is a lawyer who was wasting his life in dissipation, caught between London and Paris in a tumultuous time. His life and the lives of the other characters are sledge-hammered by the frenetic forces of the French Revolution, when the guillotine played the prominent role. Carton successfully defends in court Charles Darnay, an honorable man who looks remarkably like Carton, and thus a sort of friendship begins. Carton falls in love with Lucie Manette, but she rejects him as a less worthy person and marries Darnay instead. Through a complex succession of unjust events, Darnay finds himself flung back in prison and condemned to die at the guillotine. Sydney Carton can't get him off this time, but he sees a way to make his own life count for something, a way to give his beloved Lucie her heart's desire. Carton stands in for his double. The authorities and guards don't know they have the wrong man. Carton marches willingly to his death, and Darnay goes free. Just before the blade falls on Carton, he says these timeless words: "It is a far, far better thing that I do, than I have ever done."[1]

The scene is perhaps one of the best examples in classic literature of radical love. This kind of love has no conditions, no strings attached. It's extreme. It's self-sacrificing in the ultimate sense. It exemplifies the words of Jesus that there is no greater human love than to lay down your life for a friend.

But that story is only a shadow of the story of Jesus, who laid down His life for His enemies. That's radical love to the nth degree. The target of this book is to showcase the life of Jesus during His 1,000-day intensive ministry leading up to the real-life scene where He lays down His life, a life that was characterized all the way through by radical love. The bull's-eye of that target is that you and I become more like Jesus. Remember that He could have skipped His three-year ministry and gone straight to Calvary, except that He wanted us to see what a holy life looks like. How are you tracking so far with the aim of this book? I hope you have been watching closely as we looked at the eternal Son of God stepping into human history at Bethlehem, astounding people with His wisdom at age twelve, and launching His ministry at age thirty. Hopefully you are watching Him with growing excitement throughout His ministry years as He interacts with people. Because the more you watch Him, the more you grow to be like Him.

The outstanding characteristic of Jesus' life was His radical love. We don't have much of a picture of ordinary love in our society, let alone radical love. Maybe you have experienced precious little love of any kind in your life. Or perhaps you come from a background of abuse, and even your own father or mother didn't love you or didn't ever express love toward you. You might have been used by people you thought you could trust, and you have closed yourself off to the idea of trusting because you don't want to be hurt again. Or you simply have been jaded by the cheap portrayals of love in our culture. You know those are not accurate depictions of love, but you don't have much of a handle on what it actually is. You may understand that real love is something about placing value on another person, and you are right. That's where it starts.

And radical love—well, that is something really out there. *Radical* means "far-reaching, thoroughgoing, sweeping"; it may even be extreme in nature. Something that is radical is a departure from the norm and may even seek to change things. Have you ever seen love like that? For a while the word *radical* was adopted by the youth culture as one of their favorite superlatives, sometimes shortened to *rad*. In that sense it meant "excellent, admirable, or awe-inspiring." Have you ever seen love like that?

Well, radical love is around. Jesus demonstrated it for us. He illustrated it in the story of the good Samaritan. And get this—He wants us to act it out. Jesus never told us to do what He said; He told us to do what He did. Maybe you remember your mom or dad saying, "Don't do as I do, do as I say." Maybe they said it with a little smile, recognizing that as parents they didn't always live up to their own standards. But Jesus always lived out the way He wanted us to live.

Let's take a closer look at this kind of radical love.

Get the Last Words Before He Goes Away

When a novelist is learning to write a book, he learns that the most important words he writes will be the first line of his novel and the last. The first line has to catch the reader, acting like a hook on a fishing line. The last line is what lingers; it wraps up the story, and we take it away with us.

Jesus' last words were meant for us to take away; they rank in high importance. The incident told in Acts 1 shows Jesus ready to ascend into heaven, standing on the Mount of Olives and speaking to His followers. Then He shares His last words to His followers:

> You shall receive power when the Holy Spirit has come upon you; and you shall be witnesses to Me in Jerusalem, and in all Judea and Samaria, and to the end of the earth. (Acts 1:8)

Jesus didn't say that in a nonchalant way. He actually lived out these words. He Himself was a witness in Jerusalem, located in Judea. One instance that shows Him living out these words is His meeting with Nicodemus, a Jewish scholar, who came to Him at night and asked what all this stuff about being born again really meant. How can a man possibly be reborn? asked Nicodemus. Can he go back into his mother's womb and be born again? Jesus told him that being born again is actually imperative for entering the kingdom of God. "That which is born of the flesh is flesh, and that which is born of the Spirit is spirit. Do not marvel that I said to you, 'You must be born again'" (John 3:6–7). See, Jesus didn't just give the order for us to be witnesses in Jerusalem; He did it Himself.

Then He moved on to Samaria and came to a well, where He sat and relaxed. A woman came along, and He began talking with her about living water. He told her all the things that she had done, how she had been married many times and was living with someone now who was not her husband. She was amazed. John 4:25 says, "The woman said to Him, 'I know that Messiah is coming' (who is called Christ). 'When He comes, He will tell us all things.'" She was just kind of feeling Him out, and then Jesus said plainly, "I who speak to you am He" (John 4:26). This shows Jesus living out His own order to be a witness in Samaria.

But His order also includes the uttermost parts of the earth. Jesus never left Israel during His 1,000-day ministry, so how could He have demonstrated this? Remember the story of the nobleman in John 4, who came to Jesus and told Him his son was dying and begged for healing? The nobleman was a Roman ruler. He was not Jewish; he was from the outermost parts. Jesus told the nobleman his son was healed, which resulted in this Roman ruler becoming a believer as did all the members of his household.

Clearly, when Jesus told us to share the gospel with people in Judea and Samaria and all over the world, He didn't just say it; He did it Himself, acting in His radical love. Of course the greatest picture of His radical love was when He stretched out His arms on the cross that day on Calvary.

Romans 5:8 says, "But God demonstrates His own love toward us, in that while we were still sinners, Christ died for us." The word *still* jumps off the page because it tells us that although we are useless, lost, unlovable, and without anything to offer to God, when we were still in our sin, Jesus loved us so much that He died for us.

TAKING APART HOW RADICAL LOVE WORKS

We see radical love in action on the Jericho road, in the familiar story of the good Samaritan found in Luke 10. Jesus was with a large group of His followers and they had been celebrating a time of great victory, when a lawyer stood up to test Jesus. He was one of the crowd of religious leaders who continually tested, challenged, and baited Jesus, trying to trap Him. The word *tested* used in verse 25 is the Greek word *edpeiradzo*, which means to put through a very scrutinizing examination. The idea is to expose failure, error, or idiocy of a concept. When this lawyer stood up, it was almost an act of protest, such as we see today when people take to the streets because they don't like what's happening.

The lawyer asked Jesus, probably very piously, what he should do to inherit eternal life. Jesus answered his question with a question of His own: "Well, how do you see it? What is written in the law? How do you read it?"

The lawyer quoted scripture, and he did so accurately: "'Love the LORD your God with all your heart, with all your soul, with all your strength, and with all your mind,' and 'your neighbor as yourself'" (Luke 10:27, quoting from Deut. 6:5 and Lev. 19:18).

This man was supposed to be expert in the Old Testament law. He wasn't the kind of lawyer we are familiar with, who writes wills and does real-estate transactions and gets us out of jail. He was appointed by the scribes and Pharisees as an interpreter of the Scriptures. He was a religious lawyer.

Jesus told him that he had answered correctly and that if he could do what he had just quoted, he would live. So the lawyer replied, maybe petulantly, maybe trying to split hairs, which he was so good at, "Who is my neighbor?"

Jesus showed infinite patience with the lawyer, just as He does with you and me. He answered his question by telling him a story, one that we know as the parable of the good Samaritan:

A certain man went down from Jerusalem to Jericho, and fell among thieves, who stripped him of his clothing, wounded him, and departed, leaving him half dead. Now by chance a certain priest came down that road. And when he saw him, he passed by on the other side. Likewise a Levite, when he arrived at the place, came and looked, and passed by on the other side. But a certain Samaritan, as he journeyed, came where he was. And when he saw him, he had compassion. So he went to him and bandaged his wounds, pouring on oil and wine; and he set him on his own animal, brought him to an inn, and took care of him. On the next day, when he departed, he took out two denarii, gave them to the innkeeper, and said to him, "Take care of him; and whatever more you spend, when I come again, I will repay you." (Luke 10:30–35)

In this story we get an amazing image of what it truly means to act in radical, unconditional love. The lawyer, listening as Jesus told the story, had an agenda. He wanted to show everyone that Jesus didn't know what He was talking about, that He was dead wrong, that there were errors in Jesus' message. As the followers were celebrating victories, the lawyer stopped and said, "Hold on, wait a second." But the story Jesus told got him tangled up in his own spurious reasoning.

LIVING ON THE ROAD TO JERICHO

The story took place on the Jericho road. We may sometimes feel that we live in a place much like the Jericho road. We may be going through really difficult circumstances, and it feels as though we are traveling this rugged route alone. The Jericho road headed downward from Jerusalem. Jericho is actually northeast of Jerusalem on the map, which seems as though the road should go up. But Jerusalem is about three thousand feet above sea level, and Jericho is about one thousand feet below sea level. So this road covered a descent of about four thousand feet along extremely rough terrain.

This was a tough road to travel. It was rocky and steep, and at every turn and cranny there could be someone lying in wait ready to pounce. It was a common place to be robbed and beaten.

The Jericho road was not like most roads we travel today in our country. We jump on interstates and these are incredible roads. We can drive fast, and some of us drive even faster. There are exits along the way. If we need to use the restroom, there is a rest stop right up the road. If we are hungry, there is a sign telling us what food is available. If we are tired, we can pull off the road and spend the night in a motel or campsite. But the road to Jericho didn't have any of that kind of luxury. This was a danger zone.

Traveling on foot, the man "fell among thieves." The two words *fell among* are a translation of the Greek word *peripipto*, which means that he was surrounded by thieves. Jesus was telling us the man walked right into a trap, right into a situation where he may not make it out alive. The thieves beat him up, took all his clothing, robbed him of everything he carried, and left him for dead.

When we teach this to children, it is a favorite Bible story to act out; little boys seem to love to play the parts of the thieves and robbers. They can really get into this story. For once, they are encouraged to jump out from behind the sofa or the tree or the Sunday school screen and (at least pretend to) beat up someone.

But for the man it wasn't pretend. He was probably knocked out, and when he came to, he lay there hurting all over, bleeding and possibly having trouble breathing. Maybe panic set in. We don't know how long he lay there before he heard footsteps. They belonged to a priest who was traveling down that road. The priest saw him abandoned and in need by the side of the road, but he simply passed by on the other side. The priest seemed to do everything he could to avoid the person in need. A while later a Levite arrived at the place, walked over and glanced at the injured man, but also passed by.

The lawyer who had questioned Jesus that day had been appointed by priests and Levites. They were his bosses. He was one of their gang. They served in that gold ornate structure in the heart of Jerusalem, the temple, with its beautiful entrance, outer and inner courts, the altar where sacrifices were presented in atonement for sins, and the holy place. Behind a veil was the Holy of Holies, the place for the presence of God. The priests and Levites worked there together, to care for the temple and make sure everything was done correctly. These were the religious leaders responsible for worship.

Jesus made the point in His story that the very ones who were responsible to shepherd the people in worship of God and to portray a lifestyle that was like God were the ones who were being so unlike God. They didn't want to help the person they saw fallen and hurting. They could all talk the talk, but they didn't walk the walk. Jesus implied to the lawyer that the very people he looked up to and thought were so right all the time didn't keep the very law that he had just defined: they didn't love their neighbor.

That's when the story turned a corner. A Samaritan came along, saw the injured man, felt compassion, and helped him. Samaritans were looked at as the lowest of the low. They were awful people whom no one wanted to be around. Jews had no interest in them; they didn't socialize. Certainly priests and Levites had nothing to do with Samaritans. Who exactly were they?

In 722 BC, when the Assyrian king Sargon II took captive the Jewish people from the Northern Kingdom, he left behind the poorest and weakest and invited other nations to send people to sort of homestead land that was vacated in Israel. They brought paganism and intermarried with Jews who had been left behind. Later descendents were viewed as neither Jews nor Gentiles but held in contempt by both. The name they took comes from the city of Samaria, which had been the capital of the Northern Kingdom. In the mid-400s BC, the Samaritan governor Sanballat tried to frustrate Nehemiah's rebuilding of Jerusalem's walls. There was a complete break between Jews and Samaritans when the grandson of the high priest married Sanballat's daughter and was expelled. Sanballat built a temple for his son-in-law on Mount Gerazim. It was dedicated to the Greek god Zeus and later destroyed. In Jesus' day the entire territory between Judea and Galilee was known as Samaria, and hatred between Jews and Samaritans was at its zenith.

It is a person of this despised race whom Jesus chose to star in the story He told. The Samaritan came down that Jericho road, saw the person who had been left for dead, and felt compassion. This word *compassion* is the same Greek word used when it is said that Jesus looked out over the multitudes and saw them like sheep without a shepherd, and He was moved with compassion for them.

FINDING OUR ROLE IN THE STORY OF RADICAL LOVE

The Samaritan traveler apparently didn't hesitate. He went to the injured man, poured medicine on his wounds, bandaged them, lifted him onto his own animal, and took him to an inn where he paid for the man's care. He gave the innkeeper two denarii, two days' wages. And he told him, "Listen, if that's not enough, whatever you spend on him, I'll repay you."

Now, I have four kids, and there have been so many times when they have fallen and skinned their knees. One time Jessica ran through the house, tripped, fell, hit the corner of the doorway, and cut her head, so that was more serious. As a dad I have no problem running to my kids, getting a cloth, helping clean up wounds, dishing out Band-Aids, kissing the boo-boos—it's just something parents do. It is our instinct. But if you fall and scrape your knee, I am going to be a bit nervous about kissing your boo-boos! This Samaritan didn't even know the injured stranger, but he cared for him tenderly, sacrificially, with no strings attached. The Samaritan's actions demonstrated unconditional, radical love.

When He finished telling the story, Jesus turned to the lawyer and asked, "Which of these three do you think was neighbor to him who fell among thieves?" And the lawyer got it right. He may not have been able to bring himself to use the word *Samaritan*, but he said, "He who showed mercy on him" (Luke 10:36–37).

Jesus told him to go and do the same. Jesus made it abundantly clear that you may know the right things to do and the right words to say, but when it comes down to it, if you are faced with a person who has lost everything, someone who has been left for dead figuratively or literally, who is poor, brokenhearted, blind, or captive, that is the test of your mettle. Jesus is asking: Are you going to love this person the way I love you?

Radical love is about how we see people. The robbers saw the man on the Jericho road as a victim, a way to get what they wanted. The priests and Levites saw him as a problem to avoid. The Samaritan saw him as a person to be loved. It didn't matter if the task interfered with the Samaritan's agenda or messed up his convenience. Are we seeing people in need as Jesus would see them? Are we serving people in need as Jesus would serve them?

We need to honestly examine our hearts and ask, "If I were one of the characters in Jesus' story, which one would I be?" Surely, I am not the thief who left him for dead. Hopefully, I am not the priest or Levite. I think we all want to see ourselves as the good Samaritan.

Ask yourself, "Who am I reaching out to? Who am I sacrificing for?" It's a good idea to make a list of these people and name names. Don't be vague about it. The alternate questions we have to ask are, "Who am I passing by? Who am I pretending not to see? Who am I trying not to get involved with?"

On one wall of our church there is an account of the history of our ministry and all the incredible things God has done over a period of fifty-four years. On that wall are some handwritten notes from a sermon that my dad, Jerry Falwell, preached on September 29, 1991, a sermon he called "Investing in the Lives of Others." One statement in those handwritten notes says, "If the Christian life is anything, it is following the example of Jesus in helping hurting people."

It is a good reminder that the Christian life is not about how religious we can be. It is not about how often we attend church or how many songs we know or how many Bible verses we can recite. It has everything to do with following the example of Jesus in expressing His radical love to hurting people.

Maybe your life is best pictured by the injured man who lay by the roadside that day. Maybe you are a spiritual wreck, and you simply need Jesus to come along and pick you up. He will do that. He will do that any day anyone calls on Him.

Maybe you are a believer, but life got messed up; you are far from God and don't even remember what the excitement of serving Christ is all about. You may be going through the motions, but God's not real in your life.

Your invitation is to let Jesus pick you up and transform you into someone like Him. He is the One with the radical love.

Questions for Individual Reflection or Small Group Discussion

1. What's the most loving thing you have ever seen anyone do?
2. If someone were to ask you, "Who is your neighbor, and why should you love him?" what would you say?
3. How did the good Samaritan go above and beyond the call of duty in caring for the hurt traveler? Similarly, what sort of boundaries did the good Samaritan set in caring for the traveler—in other words, were there more things he could have done that he didn't? If so, why do you suppose he didn't do these extra things?
4. In the chapter, Jonathan poses a difficult question: We need to honestly examine our hearts and ask ourselves, "If I were one of the characters in Jesus' story, which one would I be?" How might you answer that question?
5. What does it actually mean to follow the example of Jesus in expressing His radical love to hurting people?

7

THE JAILS OF HYPOCRISY

Have you ever known a hypocrite?

Have you ever been one yourself?

I went to see a play recently in which my daughters acted. Jessica played a German nurse and wore the nurse outfit and had these little buns on the side of her head and the German accent. Natalie played a Valley Girl or some kind of brat. In the play they acted like totally different people than they really are. In essence that is a hypocrite. The word *hypocrite* comes from the first-century Greek word *hupocrites*, which means "given to the idea of an actor on a stage," actors who would wear a mask, use a script, and act out something totally different from whom they really are.

There was a whole gang of hypocrites in Jesus' day, people who did not simply act on a stage to get a story across but who lived out lives completely different from whom they were in their hearts, and Jesus had strong words for them. They acted the part of pious people who loved God when the true picture of their hearts was absolutely dark. One gang member was that lawyer who tried to trick Jesus with his questions, and Jesus responded in wisdom and told the story of the good Samaritan.

This gang of hypocrites—or any hypocrites whom you happen to meet any day and age—in your neighborhood or your church or your mirror—was the exact opposite of Jesus. If He is anything at all, Jesus is 100 percent real. He is bottom-line honest. It is a quality the Bible describes as *light*. If we are becoming more like Him, it means we are growing more real, more authentic, and more honest. We, too, gain that quality of light.

Legalism goes hand in hand with hypocrisy. *Legalism* is defined as "performing good deeds in order to gain righteousness." Legalism props up hypocrisy by convincing you that it's all about good works. If you can just perform well and keep strictly to a set of rules, you will be okay, and it doesn't matter about what is in your heart. Even in the Old Testament, God had strong words for legalists and hypocrites. He told them in Isaiah 29:13, for instance, that they could honor Him with their talk all they wanted, but He knew their hearts were far from Him.

A person may grow up in church and carry the Bible the right way and sit in the right place and be seen in the church building every time the doors open. A person may conform to a fine list of rules. But at the same time the heart can be far from God. That's a hypocrite.

This gang of hypocrites got it exactly wrong about Jesus. They watched Him cast out a demon in a man and said something like, "Oh, we get it now. Jesus can cast out demons because He is acting under the power of the devil." And they warned the crowd not to follow Jesus or listen to His words because He, they said, was Satan's servant.

Talk about backward reasoning. Jesus had had enough of this foolishness. It was time to go on the offensive and answer their nonsense. He asked them in Luke 11:14–20 how they thought Satan's kingdom could possibly stand if Satan's forces work against each other. How could the devil make any headway? He's not that stupid. It would be like a football team divided against itself with half trying to get the ball across the opposing team's goal line and the other half trying to get the ball across their own goal line.

Let's take a closer look at this practice of hypocrisy and how Jesus frees people from its jail.

MORE THAN ONE BRAND OF HYPOCRISY

Picture yourself in the crowd that day as Jesus continued teaching and got right to the heart of hypocrisy. You may feel He's put His finger on you. That's all right. That's the wonderful convicting ministry of the Holy Spirit, and it's the beginning of opening the prison doors to set you free. Jesus began to show the crowd the opposite of hypocrisy, to teach them about authenticity, about how to be real. He showed them two kinds of hypocrite: the person who appears good on the outside but hides evil in his heart and the person whose heart has been made good but who hides that goodness. That also is hypocrisy.

Jesus said, "No one, when he has lit a lamp, puts it in a secret place or under a basket, but on a lampstand, that those who come in may see the light" (Luke 11:33).

In other words, "Listen, if you've experienced the incredible light of God, you don't go and hide it—that's hypocritical." Jesus told them, essentially, that as they had been listening to Him, it was like light shining on them. When your eyes respond properly to light, you are not blind. If we are receptive to the light of Jesus' teachings, that shows we have allowed His light to penetrate and fill us, and that is something we want to share, not hide. We don't want to stuff that light into some secret place. The words *secret place* are the translation of the Greek word *krupte*. It means "a cellar or a hidden dark place."

It reminds me of our basements. We all know what basements are for, right? That is where we put all the junk that we don't want guests to see. Down in the basement is where we stuff the old TVs and remotes that don't work anymore, but you can't give them away because you paid so much for them. We have clothes down there that don't fit anymore, but we don't toss them out because maybe they have designer labels. We just have a hard time getting rid of stuff, so we cram that junk into the basement.

When guests visit, we don't generally take them to the basement. They come to the front door, where we have worked to make it look good. We didn't kick off our shoes there and throw our jackets and school bags on the floor so the entrance is a mess. If we invite someone over for dinner, we make sure the dining room looks good. We put our best furniture there and polish it up. It's not like the basement.

We might even make sure the kids clean up their bedrooms. They know what the closets are for. They open a closet, kick in all the stuff from the floor, and shut the door so the room appears tidy. The bedroom is, at least, presentable, not like the basement.

Jesus is telling us that just as we wouldn't stick our finest objects down in the cellar in a dark place, we should not take the wonderful things He gives us—love, joy, peace, and all the fruit of the Spirit—and hide them where no one can see and appreciate them. That's inauthentic. That's dishonest. That's a kind of hypocrisy.

Make sure the goodness within you is real, He cautioned, not a painted-on holiness covering a dark heart. You can make sure it is real by maintaining a good, clear spiritual eye. The eye is the gateway for light, and Jesus is the Light of the World. You don't want your spiritual eyes to be covered with cataracts. When you have physical cataracts, a film grows over your eyes so you can't see properly. Images become kind of dark and not exactly correct because your eyes are beginning to glaze over. You don't see the full and real picture. Legalism can obstruct spiritual eyesight and can deflect the light that Jesus wants to give you.

EVEN HYPOCRITES ARE GIVEN A CHANCE

We might tend to be harsh with hypocrites; surely this false front is one of the worst kinds of sins. But Jesus offered even hypocrites a chance to change. After calling a spade a spade and holding back nothing in condemning hypocrisy, Jesus was invited to dinner by a certain Pharisee. And He went! This clearly shows that no matter what kind of sin we are involved in, no matter how black our hearts are, He doesn't refuse to associate with us. We may be scarred by patterns of the basest sort of sin, but Jesus still holds out hope to us. It is possible to be so tangled in habits of hypocrisy that we hardly know when we are being real or not, but He wants to come and dine with us.

It is like the call of Matthew the tax collector, told in Matthew 9. Jesus sat down at the table in Matthew's home, and many tax collectors and other sinners came and sat with Him. The Pharisees questioned why Jesus would do such a thing, why He would eat with tax collectors and sinners. Jesus answered, "Those who are well have no need of a physician, but those who are sick. But go and learn what this means: 'I desire mercy and not sacrifice.' For I did not come to call the righteous, but sinners, to repentance" (Matt. 9:12–13).

Jesus always is ready to sit down and have a conversation with anyone who seeks Him. But watch this Pharisee who asked Jesus to dinner. He missed his big chance. Instead of welcoming Jesus and listening carefully to His every word, he was shocked because Jesus didn't wash His hands before dinner. The Pharisee is all hung up on a little rule.

In those days Pharisees and other religious leaders had this custom about meals. They had to wash their hands. And they didn't do like we do, just a quick swish or even a good soaping and rinse in a restroom before we sit down to a meal. They had a strict custom, a prescribed way to do this washing. It was a hand-washing ceremony.

Some of us make hand washing into a kind of ceremony. Some of us germophobes wash five or six times during a meal. I will admit I am hypersensitive about that. Whenever we go to a salad bar, it bothers me that after you have done your initial hand washing, you have to touch those handles that everybody else touched in order to dish up your food. Now your hands are dirty again. So usually I get my salad, bring it to the table, and wash my hands again. But to cut the restroom trips, I discreetly carry folded paper towels so that I can pick up tongs in the salad bar line with paper towels. My wife calls me weird, but you know, I never get sick!

Now the Pharisees' hand-washing ceremony was not just about germs; it was about ceremonial purification. The Pharisee who asked Jesus to dinner was shocked that He didn't perform the ceremony. Perhaps he thought that Jesus had defiled Himself by touching a Gentile.

Today in Israel you can go to the Western Wall in Jerusalem, which is all that is left of the last temple. You can walk into a restroom and find these big pitchers on a table, full of water for washing hands before worship. Each pitcher has two handles. That's so you can pour water on one hand holding one handle and then switch and pour water on the other hand holding the opposite handle. None of the filth from your hands will be there to defile you as you go and worship at the Western Wall. It has nothing to do with hygiene but everything to do with ceremonial purification. In the days of the Pharisees it had to do with making sure other people could see the performance of the religious ritual.

Jesus has a response to the person who rests all his hope in the appearance of purity. He said to His critics that day, "Now you Pharisees make the outside of the cup and dish clean, but your inward part is full of greed and wickedness. Foolish ones! Did not He who made the outside make the inside also?" (Luke 11:39–40). In no uncertain terms Jesus said that inner cleanness, cleanness of the spirit, is so much more important than outward cleanness. Jesus was asking, "Don't you get it? You Pharisees, you legalists, you hypocrites, do you know what you're doing? You're making sure that the outward looks clean, that when people look at you, everything looks good, but man, inside it is so dirty. Don't you know that the One who made you can see both outside and inside?"

Look Out—Hypocrisy Sets Traps in the Church

Before we are too hard on the Pharisees, we need to look at the problems of hypocrisy and legalism in the church today. We wear our Sunday best when we go to church, right? We take showers, dress up in our best suits and dresses, comb our hair and fix up our faces, and there is nothing wrong with all that. We are trying to show respect for God and to honor Him with our best. But in Bible times there was a custom in some cultures that those in mourning for sin and coming in confession and humility before God would actually wear sackcloth and ashes and rip their clothing. They would take that appearance to express humility before God. Maybe that's not a bad custom. We don't usually see that today, but sometimes we see someone coming into a church service wearing shorts and a T-shirt and flip-flops. We should not be shocked or look down on such people. We should celebrate that they have come to worship. Maybe that is the best they have. Or some just might not be focused on appearance or be thinking about issues of respecting God by how they look. We should welcome them happily. We should join with God in knowing that appearance isn't the thing that matters most.

The following scene happened at a posh church in an upscale neighborhood: a young woman who led a neighborhood Bible study had invited the women in that study to come to church. One was particularly resistant. We'll call her Starlight, and yes, she was a hippie. In those days the hippie subculture had spread across the land, and people who followed it tended to grow their hair long (and long beards for the men). Women wore long, baggy dresses, and both men and women wore tie-dyed T-shirts, ripped jeans, lots of beads, and often, lots of dirt. The movement rebelled against authority and renounced the establishment, and practices such as smoking marijuana and using other illegal substances and participating in so-called *free love* became rampant. To be fair, many in the movement also legitimately questioned the hypocrisy and some of the dubious values they saw in the previous generation and in the establishment. Starlight was a full-fledged hippie, into all this stuff. But she was also curious about Jesus. She came to the neighborhood study and responded to love shown to her by the women. But she worried that if she showed up at the big ritzy church, she might be asked to leave.

One day, as people gathered in the luxurious foyer before the Sunday morning service—men in suits and ties and women in fine dresses, hats, and gloves—the door opened, and Starlight walked in. She stood still and stiff and waited to see what would happen. A bit of a hush fell over the foyer. Conversing with friends, the Bible study leader noticed the hush, turned around, and saw Starlight. Without a second thought she literally ran to Starlight and threw her arms around her, knocking her own hat askew. It didn't matter that some of the dirt rubbed off on her good clothes. It didn't matter that Starlight smelled. She was welcomed. Slowly the other women of the

Bible study gathered around and welcomed Starlight also. Her heart was ready to hear God's Word, and that's all that mattered.

In 1 Samuel 15, Samuel tells Saul that God delights in obedience more than in sacrifice and that who you are in your heart is more important than your appearance. This principle was underlined when God told Samuel to go to the house of Jesse and anoint the new king. Samuel went and saw Jesse's eldest son, big and strong. Samuel was sure this must be the man. But see what God says in 1 Samuel 16:7: "Do not look at his appearance or at his physical stature, because I have refused him. For the LORD does not see as man sees; for man looks at the outward appearance, but the LORD looks at the heart." God eventually chose David, who became a man after God's own heart.

HYPOCRISY BRINGS ON WORST KINDS OF WOE

Jesus said if we want to bring on grief of the worst kind, just go ahead and be hypocrites. He pulled out all the stops, saying, "Woe to you Pharisees!" (Luke 11:42). This word *woe* is the Greek word *quai*, which literally is the idea of "great grief." The grief is right there; it's imminent, it's looming, and it pains Him. He went on to identify the worst characteristics of hypocrisy so they can change. He stripped off the masks. He laid bare five characteristics of hypocrisy that absolutely pinned them to the wall:

1. Hypocrites Value Rules over Righteousness

Jesus pointed out that instead of honest and generous giving, instead of sharing the blessings of God from an overflowing heart, they meticulously measured out a tenth of their mint and other herbs, but neglected the truly important things such as the justice and love of God. He's not saying it's wrong to tithe, but that they had left important things undone. It has been said that giving of your substance will not make you a Christian, but if you love the Lord, you will be giving of your substance. Your heart will become generous, and you won't be able to stop yourself from sharing. We so often come up with these little rules about living the Christian life, instead of just letting Jesus live it through us. The rules we create actually obstruct righteousness.

2. Hypocrites Put Reputation over Humility

If you are a hypocrite, it is all about what others are allowed to see, about making sure people like you. You want to make sure people are impressed with what you do and where you are, what kind of car you drive and what kind of career you have, and what you wear and who you hobnob with. For a hypocrite it's never about humility, about being on his knees before God, seeking His face.

In Luke 11:43, Jesus said, "Woe to you Pharisees! For you love the best seats in the synagogues and greetings in the marketplaces." Remember, we have talked about the synagogue arrangement of that day, with tiered seats on all sides. Clearly some seats were more prominent and that is where the Pharisees wanted to sit because they could be seen. Jesus said that attitude invited woe; it brought on great grief. He noted that being seen, honored, or lifted up is not important. What is important is to be humble before God.

What do we do when the Starlight at the church door is not merely dirty on the outside, but it is someone who has been involved in flagrant sin? Do we question the nerve of that person? Do we wonder how he would dare come to church after what he has done? Or do we accept that he may be coming to get right with God? Do we step completely away from whispering and gossip and welcome a sinner who was lost and now is found? We need to wrap our arms around the person who comes in humility before God because that is what Jesus does for us.

3. Hypocrites Place Popularity over Truth

Hypocrites want to be somebody. They want to be popular and be recognized for how great they are. They may even want to be recognized for what great service they do for God, but they want above all to be recognized. They want people to think they are just so awesome. Have you ever found yourself vacillating between wanting to be liked and knowing you should stand for an unpopular truth? The third and fourth characteristics of hypocrisy come from the same verse.

4. Hypocrites Think, *It's All About Me*

In Luke 11:44, Jesus said, "Woe to you, scribes and Pharisees, hypocrites!" He could have added, "You jerks!" But He said, "For you are like graves, which are not seen, and the men who walk over them are not aware of them." Those are strong words and Jesus' hearers would have understood what He meant. In those days when people were buried, graves were whitewashed to make the locations obvious. That way, people going to the temple would not step on graves. Stepping on a grave meant defilement, and it was one of their rules not to do that. Jesus was basically saying, "Do you know what you hypocrites are like? You're like those graves that no one sees, which were forgotten in the whitewashing. People who step on these graves are not aware that they are being defiled. You are just that kind of bad influence."

Then He described how hypocrites add to the burden of the law by making up more rules, but they don't follow these rules themselves.

5. Hypocrites Hinder Others from Receiving the Truth

See, the shoe was beginning to fit, and those who heard Jesus' words that day must have been getting very uncomfortable, just as we do when we are convicted. They clearly were not living according to the Old Testament scriptures and not reflecting the image of God to others. In Luke 11:52, Jesus gave a final woe, saying: "Woe to you lawyers! For you have taken away the key of knowledge. You did not enter in yourselves, and those who were entering in you hindered." The reaction of the scribes and Pharisees and lawyers was to assail Him vehemently, cross-examine Him, and lie in wait to trap Him so they could find something to accuse Him of, something that would stick. From that moment they began looking for ways to kill Him. Their reaction to conviction was, sadly, to harden in their resistance.

GET OUT OF JAIL FREE

As we close this chapter, let's ask ourselves some hard questions to make sure that we are not falling into the trap of hypocrisy, or if we have fallen, that we don't stay in the jail of hypocrisy, which is guarded by the sword of legalism.

The keys to freedom from the prison of hypocrisy are examining ourselves in humility before the Lord on these issues, repenting, and claiming His grace to change. Ask yourself these searching questions:

1. Do I value rules over righteousness? Or am I repenting where I am convicted and choosing to see and value true righteousness?
2. Do I put reputation over humility? Can I go on my face before God and tell Him honestly that He can have my reputation completely?
3. Do I put popularity over truth? Or instead, regardless of who likes me or not, do I choose to side with God's Word, and as Martin Luther said when he nailed his summary of God's truth to the church door, "Here I stand, I can do no other"?
4. Do I think life is all about me? Or can I choose to pull back from that natural self-focus and say with my whole heart, "Jesus, it's all about You"?
5. Do I hinder others from getting the truth? Can I stand aside and let God minister to the people in my life with His truth? Can I be His instrument instead of an obstacle?

These are questions we need to answer, personally, on our knees before the Lord. If the answer to any of them is yes, then the solution is found in Jesus. He frees us from the jails of hypocrisy and invites us to authenticity and truth.

Questions for Individual Reflection or Small Group Discussion

1. Have you ever known a hypocrite? Have you ever been one yourself? What did the situation look like?
2. What is legalism, and how does legalism go hand in hand with hypocrisy?
3. How is hiding "light"—in other words, hiding peace, love, joy, and other fruits of the Holy Spirit—a form of hypocrisy?
4. Jesus showed a deliberate anger and harshness whenever He interacted with hypocrites. Why might the display of a false front be one of the worst kinds of sin?
5. Jonathan asks five difficult and heart-probing questions at the end of this chapter. How did you, personally, answer the questions, and how is the solution to these questions found in Jesus?

8

THE PARADOXICAL
HAPPINESS OF *LESS*

oward Hughes was an eccentric movie and airline baron who
amassed a fortune of cash, holdings, and properties worth
billions of dollars in the early part of the twentieth century.
The story is told that someone asked him near the end of his life,
"How much does it take to make a man happy?" Hughes paused
thoughtfully, then replied, "Just a little more."

We may not have billions or millions or even a little cash-cushion
in the bank, but regardless of our economic level, we generally think
we'll be happier with more. During Jesus' 1,000-day ministry He
spent time teaching us a paradoxical truth: that we can actually be
happier with less. As we look at His life and come to understand His
mind on this subject, we'll truly come to know Him better than we
have ever known Him before. As we come to know Him we become
more like Him and enter into that contentment and rest of spirit that
He promised. That's the whole point of looking at these 1,000 days.

The mind-set of contentment in our age of consumerism may
sound strange, maybe impossible, but Jesus underscores it, first by
warning us about the opposite, the mind-set of greed. In Luke 12:15,
Jesus said, "Take heed and beware of covetousness." That word
covetousness is *pleonexia* in the Greek language, which means "an
insatiable, inordinate desire to want more and more."

Does that sound like the culture in which we live? We may not
call it covetousness but the same urge is in action all around us today.
Covetousness is one of the major operating principles of our society.

If we turn on the television to watch sports, we are going to view a number of commercials throughout the game, right? They are going to tell us about a certain kind of soft drink we absolutely must buy, what kind of sports shoes we need to wear, and even what we should use to brush our teeth. They are going to insist that we absolutely cannot live without all this stuff.

The overall effect of watching commercial after commercial produces the intended results. Do you ever find yourself listening and watching, and suddenly you get this insatiable desire to have whatever is being sold? You can picture yourself wearing it or using it or driving it, and soon you are starting to figure out how you can squeeze it into your budget.

Our desire to get more and more of everything is fed constantly. We find ourselves running in the mode of need it, want it, gotta have it.

But is that truly best for our lives?

Jesus invites us to a better way of living. Let's explore more of His teaching in this chapter.

I've Got to Get What's Due Me

Jesus gave this warning against covetousness at a large gathering where He was teaching. He gave encouragement about being faithful to truth and reassurance that God will care for us in the face of whatever fears might be around the corner. He encouraged us to focus on the things that last forever. This important teaching was interrupted by a man who was focused on the here and now and all the stuff he could get.

People were pressed shoulder to shoulder, trying to hear the important truths Jesus was teaching, and one person interrupted Him, making a demand straight out of left field: "Teacher, tell my brother to divide the inheritance with me" (Luke 12:13). It's as if he dismissed all Jesus' teaching about eternal things and said, "That's all fine and good, but so what? I need You to tell my brother to give me my money and do it now." Back in those days the older brother received a double portion of the family inheritance, and he was responsible to care for that inheritance for the entire family. This man who interrupted Jesus was obviously a younger brother wanting what he saw as his chunk of the loot. He as much as said, "I don't care what You're talking about, Jesus. I don't care about all this teaching on hypocrisy and truth and numbering of hairs on a person's head. I just want my cash."

There are perhaps no disputes more bitter than when family members fight over an inheritance. We see occasions of it all the time. Siblings who formerly got along with each other hear the reading of the will of their last parent, and everything hits the fan. Somebody feels slighted, passed over, or like dad always loved the other one best. Lawyers are called in who end up with most of the money, and precious relationships are broken, all because of an inheritance dispute like the one brought to Jesus that day.

Notice that Jesus refused to arbitrate the situation because that was not the heart of the matter. He focused on the man's real need, saying, "Take heed and beware of covetousness." And He added this important statement: "For one's life does not consist in the abundance of the things he possesses" (Luke 12:15).

Jesus was trying to get the young man (and the rest of us, for that matter) to understand that life is not all about stuff. He could look ahead and see that in our time, our culture would shout the opposite message every day. He knew all about the pressure that would come down on us to get the latest stuff, the best stuff, and to shop till we drop.

It might be a new electronic gadget that you think you need, maybe a newer model car even though the old one works fine, or a new set of clothes that puts last season's colors together in a slightly different way. Some suspect that products are actually manufactured with built-in obsolescence so they will break down in a short time. Then we will have to replace them, keep spending, and keep the economy ticking. Even in the grocery store the pressure builds. We walk down the aisles and see product after product marked "new and improved" or words to that effect. We open magazines and the brain-washing jumps off the pages at us. We are given pictures of what a fabulous life we can have if we just own—*whatever*. We become convinced that a certain experience will be generated by owning a certain object and we will evolve into the person we really want to be. We get into huge problems because we spend beyond our means, both as individuals and as nations. Jesus was telling us that life is not all about stuff.

The young man in our story apparently knew that Jesus was somebody special, for he called Him "Teacher," that is, a person of wisdom. The man had come that day to the gathering with the intention of listening to Jesus. But he allowed his mind to wander to the fight with his brother over the inheritance. And he stopped concentrating. He stopped hearing the important things Jesus was saying. Whenever we allow stuff to become more important to us than anything else, our ears grow deaf to the truth.

BEWARE THE BIG BAD WOLF OF COVETOUSNESS

Watch out for this terrible greed; it will eat you up. Covetousness will give you just the opposite of the happiness it promises. Jesus used a strong phrase in Luke 12:15: "Take heed." That's a translation of the Greek word *horao*, which means "to look, to open your eyes." He added another strong word, *beware*, a translation of the Greek word *phulasso*, which means "to guard against, to put protections in place." Jesus was telling this man and telling you and me to open our eyes and put guards around ourselves, protect ourselves from this insatiable, inordinate desire for more and more stuff because it will destroy us.

I hope my son will forgive me for using this story, but it perfectly illustrates this point. Years ago when Jonathan Jr. was just a little boy, my family was going out for dinner with my parents. Jonathan had recently graduated from baby food into regular food, and he had this incredible appetite for french fries. We would go to a restaurant, and he would say, "I want french fries and a side order of french fries, please." He just had to have them.

We walked into this restaurant together that day, gave the hostess the number in our party, and had to wait awhile. Jonathan was hungry and said, "Dad, I don't want to wait. I want food now. Let's go to McDonald's. They've got good french fries." I reassured him it would be fine, and sure enough after a while the hostess came and led us to our table. Dad led, and we all followed, and Jonathan was kind of lagging behind. It turned out that he was busy. As he passed tables where people already had their food, he reached onto their plates and helped himself to french fries all along the way. He picked up french fry after french fry after french fry. We didn't see it until my mom turned around and caught him in the act. People were sitting there kind of stunned, some amused, but some with faces that said, "I can't believe this kid!"

We laughed about it later, but I realized this is something we all do. We walk through life and see the stuff other people have, and we want it. And we don't want to wait for it. We burn with an insatiable desire to get more and more, so we go out and buy things we can't afford. We walk through life picking up everything we can grab because we have this urge that tells us life is all about stuff.

That's not you or me, though, is it? We don't have too much; actually we just need a little bit more and we'll be fine, right? I don't know the net financial worth of the young man who tried to get Jesus to arbitrate the family estate dispute, but he undoubtedly thought he needed more. Jesus was patient with him and, as He did so often, used a parable to try to teach the man what is truly important:

> The ground of a certain rich man yielded plentifully. And he thought within himself, saying, "What shall I do, since I have no room to store my crops?" So he said, "I will do this: I will pull down my barns and build greater, and there I will store all my crops and my goods. And I will say to my soul, 'Soul, you have many goods laid up for many years; take your ease; eat, drink, and be merry.'" But God said to him, "Fool! This night your soul will be required of you; then whose will those things be which you have provided?" (Luke 12:16–20)

This farmer had a bumper crop; he apparently couldn't sell it all and didn't have enough bin-space to store it in. *No problem*, he thought, *I'll just tear down the little old bins and build supersized bins; I'll amass as much as possible; then I'll keep going and build more warehouses to protect all my stuff, and I'll just go out and party.* It reminds us of actor Charlie Sheen, who reportedly made almost two million dollars for each episode of his most recent sitcom.[1] We all would like that, wouldn't we? Well, we think we would, but the problem is, if we got two million dollars a week, we still would not be happy. Look at where Charlie Sheen's wealth has landed him.

The Delusion of Greed

In the parable God stopped this farmer in his tracks. Jesus is cautioning us, "Hold on. What if you die tonight? Then who will all your stuff belong to?" None of us are more than a heartbeat away from eternity. Jesus said the farmer is just like anyone who is focused on stuff instead of the things that will last forever. Luke 12:21 says, "So is he who lays up treasure for himself, and is not rich toward God." The man in the parable was deluded by greed. He began to think that he could control his life. He talked to himself in a self-satisfied way, and told his soul that he deserved a little R&R time, now that he had all this wealth stored up as a hedge against future disaster. Independently wealthy, he could live in the style to which he'd become accustomed long into the future. So he thought. But he was deluded.

The first thing he missed: we are not promised tomorrow. Life is fragile and can be snuffed out at any moment. The second thing he missed: stuff is never secure. Wealth is never absolute. No investment is risk free. Thieves, moths, rust, inflation, job loss, unexpected expenses, economic recession—these are just a few of the things that threaten our wealth. Possessions are fleeting. They come and go. We have seen that big time these last few years in the world economy. The stock market is up and down. Oil prices are low and then high. Money and possessions are easy come, easy go. Here is the truth that rips the delusion off greed: possessions are not the important thing; they have absolutely no spiritual value.

We simply can't base our lives on the things we own. We see

the parable played out today when people rest their security on their bank account balances, the stocks they hold, the houses they live in, the cars they drive, or the labels they wear. But whether all the stuff stays or goes, they are not happy. Because having stuff is not what makes us rich; knowing God makes us rich.

In the Old Testament we find the story of Solomon, the wisest and richest man who ever lived. This guy had it all. He was smart and he was savvy. He had a great store of information and the wisdom to interpret his information. He had all the money you could possibly imagine. And he had power. He was the king. If you wrote out a list of everything you could possibly want, this guy had it. But look at what he wrote: "He who loves silver will not be satisfied with silver; nor he who loves abundance, with increase" (Eccl. 5:10).

Solomon made the point that stuff doesn't satisfy. He blasted the big delusion of greed: it promises contentment but simply doesn't deliver. This man, the wisest man who ever lived (next to Jesus), was saying, "No matter how much stuff you get—more stuff, bigger stuff, better stuff, brand-new stuff—it will never make you happy."

TURNING AROUND THE DELUSION OF GREED

The delusion of greed insists that if we get just a little more, we will be happy. The truth turns that idea on its head. The truth is that acquiring stuff has nothing to do with happiness. In fact, we may actually be happier with less. This is a cultural upheaval. Jesus did not say that simply being poor will make you happy. He said the riches that will make you happy are spiritual, not material. We will be more able to focus on riches of the spirit if our material lives are stripped down and made a little simpler.

To turn greed upside down, we must first face three facts:

1. Control of life and death is in God's hands, and we need to lay down the notion that we have anything to say about it. We are never promised tomorrow or even one more minute. It helps us hold our material goods loosely if we know we may be parted

from them without a moment's notice. Remember, you can't take it with you.

2. Material wealth is in God's hands. It can come and go as quickly as snapping your fingers. Part of the reason God gives us material blessings is so we'll have something to share. It's not hard to look around and find people in need, often in our own neighborhoods, or places around the world that have been hit hard by disasters. There are many people who can use a helping hand, and the poorest of us in this country has something to share.

3. Our part is to live in thankfulness. So often we focus on the provisions instead of God the provider. We spend a lot of time working for stuff, researching stuff, buying stuff, hauling stuff home, storing stuff, cleaning stuff, sorting stuff, repairing stuff, getting rid of stuff so we can replace it with other stuff, and we get all wound up in this cycle of stuff. Some of this is necessary, of course, but we want to always look behind the stuff and remember where it comes from and simply be thankful to God who provides.

There is no merit in calling material stuff evil. It is our attitudes that Jesus was dealing with. Life is more than food and more than clothes. Jesus said this clearly in Luke 12:24: "Consider the ravens, for they neither sow nor reap, which have neither storehouse nor barn; and God feeds them. Of how much more value are you than the birds?" Jesus pointed out that these wild birds don't have jobs or bank accounts or warehouses to keep their stuff. They don't get inheritances from their parents or social security or pensions. Yet they are God's creatures and He feeds them.

Jesus made the point that we can't even add a little bit to our height if we should want to, so if we can't do these little things, why worry about adding to our storage bins? To the listening crowd, most of whom probably had trouble making ends meet, to the young man fighting with his brother, to you and to me, Jesus said these immortal words:

Consider the lilies, how they grow: they neither toil nor spin; and yet I say to you, even Solomon in all his glory was not arrayed like one of these. If then God so clothes the grass, which today is in the field and tomorrow is thrown into the oven, how much more will He clothe you, O you of little faith? (Luke 12:27–28)

He told us not to be anxious about food and clothing and necessities, not to be constantly on the hunt, as people are all over the world. Why not? How can we be assured of having what we need if we don't scramble and claw after it? Simply, "Your Father knows that you need these things" (Luke 12:30). That ought to be enough information to calm our fears about necessities. Pointing to how God provides for lilies and birds is not meant to encourage laziness. They are not able to plant crops or sew clothing. God intends for us to use the abilities He gave us, not to live as though working and acquiring stuff are all there is to life.

FORTUNE HUNTING FOR THE RIGHT TREASURE

Since happiness is clearly not in getting more stuff, Jesus told us where true happiness lies: "Seek the kingdom of God, and all these things shall be added to you" (Luke 12:31). Put your focus and attention on Jesus, on growing more like Him, and all the material stuff you actually need will be looked after.

We are all gold diggers in some ways; we are all fortune hunters. Jesus knows that we have this instinct to get things, and it is not all bad if we let Him turn it around for us. He told us exactly how to do that. He told us to pay attention to what kind of fortune we are seeking and where our fortune is stored. Because, He said, "Where your treasure is, there your heart will be also" (Luke 12:34). Someone has said, you can't take it with you but you can send it on ahead.

Ask yourself this searching question: "Where is my treasure?" The answer is surely not a list of assets and liabilities, bank account numbers and safety deposit box keys. The question is, what do you value more than anything else? Where is it kept? When you can answer that question, you'll know where your heart is. It could be caught up in sports; it could be caught up in your job. Maybe relationships are the most important thing to you, even more important than God. Our hearts can be caught up in a myriad of things, big things or trivial things. We simply need to make sure we are rich toward God, that our treasure is found in our relationship with almighty God.

Maybe your foundations feel shaken by the twin volcanoes of hypocrisy and greed that we have discussed in the last two chapters. Maybe you have seen as never before that, yes, this awful stuff is inside your own heart. You are a sinner, and you know it, and you are not sure if your sin has ever been handled. This would be a good time to ask yourself, carefully, slowly, searchingly, if you have ever brought all this baggage to the Savior. We all have the baggage of sin. But the good news is that there is forgiveness, offered through Jesus.

It works like this: Jesus took the punishment for all our sins when He died an *infinite* death on the cross. The events of history were that God the Son lived on the earth, died on the cross at Calvary, was buried, and rose from the grave three days later to show He conquered death. He went through all that because He loves His creatures just that much. And don't worry that the death of one person wasn't enough to substitute for all of us. God the Son was big enough to take upon Himself all the sins of anyone who has ever lived or ever will live. His death was big enough to cancel all those sins. It applies to anyone who will put their trust in Him. All we must do is agree with God that this wonderful work of Jesus on the cross can be applied to us. We can just say to Him something like, "Jesus, I surely do know that I am a sinner. And I understand You died on the cross to take away sins. That's certainly all right with me! I really appreciate it, and I thank You with all my heart."

A simple prayer like that can create a moment in which you pass from death into life. You become a Christian, and forgiveness is yours, now and for all eternity. It is the beginning of leaving hypocrisy, greed, and all the garbage behind and starting on the life that is characterized by contentment. In the next chapter we are going to deal with some hard stuff. This is stuff you don't want to look at unless you have the assurance that you are one of God's children through faith in Jesus Christ. Make this your moment. Speak your prayer of surrender to Him before you turn the page.

Questions for Individual Reflection or Small Group Discussion

1. What examples of covetousness and greed have you seen in the culture around you? How might you have seen these undesirable traits in your own life?

2. Have you ever approached God with a request or even a demand about a physical need, while at the same time pushing aside Jesus' emphasis about eternal things? What did the situation look like?

3. In the parable of the rich man who wanted to build bigger barns, what was the mistake he made?

4. "If we get just a little more, we'll be happy." What do you think of this sentence? Can it ever be true? Can it ever be false?

5. What does Jesus say is the answer to always wanting more?

9

GOOD NEWS/BAD NEWS

A Christian construction worker had been sharing his faith with fellow workers during a break. A burly fellow raised an eyebrow, pulled open the tab on his beer, and chugged it down. Then he said loudly, "Well, I'll tell you this. Hell is the place I'm going, and that's fine with me. All my friends will be there, and we're going to party hard." And his roar of laughter led the others as they returned to their picks and shovels. The Christian thought about that with an aching heart as he labored beside the others through the afternoon. Did his fellow worker make a good point? No, he concluded. If there were any truth to the picture, if there were any place where a person could party or feel any kind of comradeship with friends, it wouldn't be in hell.

When it comes to good news and bad news, there is no more extreme truth than the news about heaven and hell. Life on earth isn't all there is. It is a trial run for eternity, and Jesus was always clear that every person will be in one of these two locations in a never-ending experience. Jesus talked about these realities during His 1,000 days of ministry. He spent a lot of time teaching about what happens to us after we die, after we leave this life. He didn't answer every question we might want to ask about heaven and hell, but He taught us all we really need to know to ensure that we go to the right place.

Before we consider Jesus' teachings on heaven and hell, let's look at some things He did not teach. He did not teach anything about a bright tunnel or a white light. He did not teach soul sleep, a belief that people just go to sleep spiritually when they die and stay asleep until judgment or, alternatively, that they sleep forever. He did not teach that there is a limbo or purgatory or any kind of intermediate place. He did not teach that we go someplace and get punished for a while until our sins are fully paid for and only then do we go into His presence. He did not teach that there is a nirvana or that we are reincarnated as bugs or animals or other people. He did not teach annihilationism—the idea that the soul is just wiped out or sucked up into the universe. He did not teach that anyone just disappears into nothingness because He created us all to be everlasting beings. He did not teach universalism, the belief that everybody is eventually taken to heaven, because that would cancel the point of the cross, and all the warnings Jesus gave about hell would be meaningless. He did not teach that we just kind of hang out in the clouds somewhere.

Actually, Jesus didn't talk about the afterlife, a term used commonly today; He talked about eternal life and eternal death. We can understand this more clearly if we realize that death is simply separation. There are three kinds of death, and each has to do with a specific kind of separation:

1. Physical death occurs when the soul-spirit is separated from the body. Perhaps you have stood at the graveside of a loved one and realized that your loved one was not really there. That body, placed into the ground, was only a shell. The soul-spirit had already been separated from the body.
2. Spiritual death describes the separation of the soul-spirit from God, and that is the state people are in if they are without the Savior. They might still be walking around, but they are spiritually dead.
3. Eternal death is simply the state of spiritual death continuing forever.

These are the clear names Jesus gave to these truths, rather than vaguely talking about an afterlife. So let's take a closer look at what Jesus actually taught about what happens when we die.

TEMPORARY HEAVEN AND HELL

In today's culture there are many Christians, even pastors, who are unwilling to talk about hell. It is not a popular teaching because it doesn't make people feel good. But hell is a fact just as heaven is a fact, and we are wise if we look at what Jesus taught about them.

First, He taught that there are a temporary heaven and a temporary hell. That's not as hard to understand as it may seem at first. Jesus acknowledged that there are temporary places for heaven and hell, which will issue in permanent places for heaven and hell. The people who are in heaven or hell today are not in the same places that they will be for eternity. The places they are in now have the same characteristics and nature, but they are not the same as the forever heaven and hell.

Hades, *death*, and *Sheol* are the names given in the Bible to the temporary hell. Let's picture it this way: you have been justly convicted of a crime, and you are on your way to the penitentiary, but there is no room for you yet. That new prison is still being built. So you are kept in a holding cell. You are locked up with freedom denied to you. The holding cell has the same nature as the penitentiary, but it is not the same place. When the penitentiary is ready, your sentence is commuted to it, and you are transferred to the big house. So people today who die without Christ don't go to the lake of fire. They are kept in the holding cells of the place referred to as *Hades*, *death*, or *Sheol*. Someday they will be commuted to the lake of fire, known as *Gehenna* or hell proper.

It is the same way with heaven. Let's say you are planning to move to Chicago. You landed a new job, you have friends and family waiting for you there, and you are building a beautiful new home in the suburbs. Your home is still under construction when you need to make your move. So you get a temporary apartment. It's a nice place; maybe it has a swimming pool and a great view, and you enjoy it thoroughly, but it is not your permanent home.

The Bible calls the temporary heaven "paradise" or "Abraham's bosom." Abraham was the father of the faithful, so God uses his name to signify the place where people go to await their permanent home in heaven. Jesus gives us more details about these temporary places in a story found in Luke's gospel.

HELL: A NOT-SO-PRETTY PICTURE

Jesus was teaching one day about hell and directed this teaching straight at the Pharisees, who had set themselves against Him. He told the story of a rich man and a beggar named Lazarus. It is unknown if this actually happened or if it was a parable, a term used for the fictional illustrations Jesus told to get across specific truths. In His parables Jesus typically didn't give names to the characters, but He did in this story, so it very well could be an actual event. Certainly this is a picture God wants us to get.

Luke 16:19–21 says, "There was a certain rich man who was clothed in purple and fine linen and fared sumptuously every day. But there was a certain beggar named Lazarus, full of sores, who was laid at his gate, desiring to be fed with the crumbs which fell from the rich man's table. Moreover the dogs came and licked his sores."

This was the situation when these two people were still alive on earth. The rich man was—well—rich. He had a beautiful place, all the comforts, all the food he could eat and some to waste. He threw big parties. He was surrounded by all the right people. He lived a life of ease and was not prone to sharing. The beggar, Lazarus, was by any definition, poor. He was diseased and had to beg to keep body and soul together. He lay outside the gate every day, outside the rich man's house, hoping for just a morsel of food. Nobody cared for him. He was all alone. It became so bad that street dogs came along to lick his sores and pester him. Two different men, two different lifestyles, but their situations were about to change.

Luke 16:22–23 says, "So it was that the beggar died, and was carried by the angels to Abraham's bosom. The rich man also died and was buried. And being in torments in Hades, he lifted up his eyes and saw Abraham afar off, and Lazarus in his bosom."

Pause the story a moment to just picture the situation. Their fortunes have been reversed. The two men both died, but Lazarus, whom nobody cared about in life, died and was carried by angels. Yes, angels. This was his first taste of heaven. He was accompanied by beings who love and care for him because that's how it is in heaven. We are with God's family. The rich man, by contrast, died, and Jesus just says he was buried. Maybe nobody even came to the funeral. Maybe he was mean and alone like Ebenezer Scrooge at the beginning of Dickens's *A Christmas Carol*. In life, the rich man had only fair-weather friends, groupies who hung around hoping some of his riches would rub off. But the rich man died, woke up, and found himself in torment. Notice that he was awake and aware, in a body that was able to feel pain and torment. He could thirst but could get no relief. He suffered but was not able to go into a death-like oblivion. He had thoughts about what's going on back on earth. He had memory. He saw Lazarus standing beside Abraham in heaven. What's he going to do?

> Then he cried and said, "Father Abraham, have mercy on me, and send Lazarus that he may dip the tip of his finger in water and cool my tongue; for I am tormented in this flame." But Abraham said, "Son, remember that in your lifetime you received your good things, and likewise Lazarus evil things; but now he is comforted and you are tormented. And besides all this, between us and you there is a great gulf fixed, so that those who want to pass from here to you cannot, nor can those from there pass to us." (Luke 16:24–26)

He went on to ask Father Abraham to send Lazarus to his old home and warn his five brothers about hell, but he is told that they have the writings of Moses and the prophets to warn them. The once-rich man knew they hadn't listened to Moses and the prophets just as he didn't, and he pleaded that if someone were to come back from the dead to warn them, they would surely pay attention. But Father Abraham told him, "If they do not hear Moses and the prophets, neither will they be persuaded though one rise from the dead" (Luke 16:31).

The rich man basically had two requests. When he looked up to heaven, it's almost as if he pictured a ladder and thought Lazarus could climb down it to him. He asked Abraham to send the former beggar to him with a drink of water. That's all he wanted. Notice he didn't ask for forgiveness or for mercy. He didn't ask to speak to God and say, "I'm sorry, God, I should not have lived the way I did." He was still thinking about himself. He asked for someone to come and care for his comforts. But it didn't work. Abraham told him there is no ladder from heaven to hell; he can't send Lazarus down. He told the man, "You are where you are, and he is where he is, and that's that."

So the rich man tried another tactic. Maybe there was some way Lazarus could get from heaven to earth. The rich man's second request was for Abraham to send Lazarus to warn his brothers. Abraham told him that was also impossible. There is no ladder from heaven to earth. Besides, the rich man's brothers have already had the warnings of all the Old Testament scriptures and haven't paid attention, so even if someone came back from the dead, they would ignore him.

It seems that Jesus was giving them a hint, doesn't it? He hinted about His own resurrection and predicted that even when that wonderful act became history, people could choose not to believe. Instead, they could choose hell.

HELL: MORE THAN A CARTOON OR AN INFERNO

Popular culture often pictures hell as kind of a comical stoked-up furnace tended by little red men with tails and horns running around with pitchforks, and it's all a joke. People dress up like creatures of hell on Halloween and even dress children in devil costumes and think it's cute.

We get another quite different picture of hell from the classic poet Dante Alighieri, who wrote in the fourteenth century. In his poem *Inferno*, the first part of a longer poem called *Divine Comedy*, he tells of a journey through the medieval concept of hell. Hell is shown as nine concentric circles of the worst kind of suffering the human mind can imagine. Sinners are punished with specific consequences appropriate to the type of sin. The tortures range from consuming maggots to tormenting fire. The final gate into hell bears the inscription, "Abandon every hope, all you who enter."

Dante doesn't trivialize hell, and he sees sin for the horror that it is. Although his poem has done much to warn people through the centuries of the terrors of hell, it is not Scripture and not completely accurate.

The Bible gives us the accurate picture of hell, and it also is not pretty. The Bible indicates that hell is a real place where real people spend a real eternity with real bodies. We'd rather skip these parts of the Bible. People in today's culture have a hard time dealing with this. We think that somehow a God of love wouldn't talk about hell. And surely a Jesus of grace wouldn't send anybody to hell. But Jesus didn't avoid the subject. He described hell in words about fire and torment, tears and suffering, darkness and loneliness. He mentioned hell twelve times. He talked about fire and furnace nine times. He referred to judgment more than twenty times. He mentioned Hades twice. He spoke of weeping and wailing and gnashing of teeth seven times. He spoke of eternal punishment four times. By these words Jesus strongly warned people: this is a place you do not want to go.

In Luke 13, He gave us another picture similar to the story of the rich man and Lazarus. God is shown as telling people who rejected Him that He doesn't know them or where they come from. He tells these evildoers to get away from Him. He uses the phrase "Depart from Me" or "Away from Me" (Luke 13:27). Those three words may be the most accurate description of hell in the entire Bible. In a nutshell, they tell us what hell is. Hell is a place where we are away from God.

Jesus added that there will be weeping and gnashing of teeth when those who rejected Him see Abraham, Isaac, Jacob, and all the prophets, but they themselves are outside that blessed place. They will be in a place away from God, and that is what hell is.

With all the warnings Jesus gave, why are there people still heading to hell? We don't know the full answer to this mystery. But we do know that God tells us clearly people are in hell because of the sovereign holiness of God and the selfish rebellion of the wicked. Let's be clear: people who go to hell choose to do so.

God's Word declares that He is holy and requires holiness from us, and He has provided a way for us to become holy. But if a person rejects the way, rejects the death and resurrection of Jesus, then that person is choosing not to be with God. If we don't want Him as Savior and king during this short earth experience, we certainly don't want Him throughout eternity. The only other place you can go if you don't want to be with a holy God is the place built for the devil and his demons. People go to hell because they decide to. They are those who shake their fists in God's face and say, "I won't have You as ruler over me."

C. S. Lewis once said that hell is a place where the gates are barred from the inside. This may or may not be technically true, but Lewis was making the point that hell is a place where people are by choice. It's as if God says to a rebel, "Okay, not My will but yours be done. You want to walk away from Me. I've done everything I can do for you. But if this is what you want, if you don't want to be with Me, there's only one other place for you. Go ahead—go to the place that is away from Me."

This is not a harsh, vindictive Jesus who spoke these words about hell. In the same chapter, we see Him brokenhearted, weeping over Jerusalem, His beloved city, and its people who killed the prophets and stoned the messengers God sent to them. And He spoke these tender words: "How often I wanted to gather your children together, as a hen gathers her brood under her wings, but you were not willing!" (Luke 13:34).

HEAVEN: MORE THAN A RIDE ON A CLOUD

You have probably seen the pictures of heaven that are pushed by popular culture, pictures that are trivial, boring, or sentimentally sugar-sweet. Rest assured, it is not likely that we will float around on clouds strumming harps or eating cream cheese. The truth is that heaven is essentially the good side of this good news/bad news scenario. The good news about heaven starts with this simple truth: no one has to go to hell. We don't have to pay for our own sin in either a holding cell or the penitentiary. Instead, God has prepared a place called heaven for those who trust Him.

Heaven is a real place where real people spend a real eternity in real bodies. Are there golden streets and pearly gates in heaven? Yes, the Bible speaks of these. There are probably no words in human language to describe exactly how wonderful heaven is, so Bible writers used the best pictures they could come up with. Heaven is described not as a ghostly place but a solid and wonderful reality.

Imagine waking up one morning and finding your life has no stress, no pressure, no sin, no prodigal experiences, no broken marriages, no diseases, no need for medications, no side effects, no bills to pay, no bankruptcy, no loneliness, no suffering. Are you up for something like that?

When Jesus spoke about heaven, He used language that describes banquets, feasts, and family. He talked of friends and closest fellowship. It is apparently a place of eternal activity but also of eternal rest from all cares. When Jesus was dying on the cross, the thief dying next to Him clearly trusted Jesus and asked to be remembered in His kingdom. Jesus turned to him and said, "Assuredly, I say to you, today you will be with Me in Paradise" (Luke 23:43).

Jesus used *paradise* as one of the names for the temporary heaven. *Paradise*, in the original language, means the "park or the garden of the king." Some Bible students tie that to the garden of Eden. Maybe heaven is a little like that garden before the fall because it was a perfect place, created for people to enjoy God's presence and take care of the earth, naming and nurturing things. Maybe heaven is the garden of Eden rebooted. Maybe heaven is paradise found. But whatever it is exactly, we know heaven is the place where Jesus is.

Near the end of Jesus' 1,000-day ministry, His friends asked Him about heaven. To comfort and encourage them He said, "Let not your heart be troubled; you believe in God, believe also in Me. In My

Father's house are many mansions; if it were not so, I would have told you. I go to prepare a place for you. And if I go and prepare a place for you, I will come again and receive you to Myself; that where I am, there you may be also" (John 14:1–3).

If we were to ask Jesus, "What's heaven all about?" He would say, "It's all about being with Me." Yes, it's beautiful and spectacular, but the main thing is that Jesus is there. Nothing about heaven will be frightening because Jesus will be there.

BEST DAY EVER FOREVER

To get a handle on heaven in your mind, think about your best day ever. Picture a day that was just super, a day you had wished would never end, a day when you lost all track of time. Maybe it was a summer day riding bikes with your family, eating deep-dish pizza, and talking with easy communication about important things. It could have been a day in the old family home surrounded by corn fields, cooking a barbecue meal, with kids running around with sparklers and everyone laughing together. Or a day when you were ministering to a group of children who responded to the love of Jesus and had smiles from ear to ear.

Picture your own personal best day ever and then imagine it never ending. That gives us a little taste of heaven. It is a place where Jesus and His family work together and laugh and sing and dance and write and create and build and learn and continue on forever. It never ends because there is no time. And it never gets boring because there's no time factor to take the edge off that first fresh taste of wonder.

Heaven is not about wings and halos and clouds. Picture the most beautiful scene you have ever looked at; heaven is more beautiful. Imagine the most glorious blend of your favorite colors anyone could ever put together; heaven is more glorious. Think of the most fun you could possibly have, the most interesting thing you could do, the most exciting thrill, the most rewarding experience; heaven is way beyond all that. Picture the place where you are together with Jesus, the One who loves you the most, and there is never any need to say good-bye. That is heaven.

Remember that Jesus warned there is no ladder between heaven and hell or from heaven to earth. But it turns out there is a sort of ladder from earth to heaven. Remember Jacob from the Old Testament? Genesis 28 tells us that one night he was sleeping under the open sky and had a dream where he saw a ladder with angels going up and down it. Jesus cleared up the mystery of what that ladder meant. In John 1, an incident is recorded where a young man named Nathaniel told Jesus he was just amazed at the wonders Jesus was doing. Jesus smiled and told him, "Hold on, Nathaniel, you haven't seen anything yet."

He told Nathaniel that one day he would see angels ascending and descending, not on a ladder but on the Son of Man (a name Jesus gave Himself). In other words, Jesus is the ladder. Jesus is the way from earth to heaven. In fact, He is the only way. When His friends were wondering about how to find the way to heaven, Jesus told them in John 14:6, "I am the way, the truth, and the life. No one comes to the Father except through Me."

Let's close this chapter this way—by asking yourself what you can do with this information. Really, it is three things. As you think about eternity, spent either in heaven or in hell, contemplate the following truths:

1. Make sure you yourself are on the way to heaven. Make sure you have claimed for yourself the good news about heaven and how to get there.
2. Study these wonderful truths about heaven and warnings about hell; grasp them firmly in your mind, in order to prepare yourself for conversations with friends.
3. Pray for people within your circle of influence who are headed the wrong direction, and pray for the door to open for conversations about the eternal truths of heaven and hell.

QUESTIONS FOR INDIVIDUAL REFLECTION OR SMALL GROUP DISCUSSION

1. If a friend of yours said something like this to you—"Well, I'll tell you this. Hell is the place I'm going, and that's fine with me. All my friends will be there and we're going to party hard"—what would you say, and why?

2. What are some of the things people commonly believe about what happens to them when they die?

3. Jonathan makes this strong statement about hell: "With all the warnings Jesus gave, why are there people still heading to hell? We don't know the full answer to this mystery. But we do know that God tells us clearly people are in hell because of the sovereign holiness of God and the selfish rebellion of the wicked. Let's be clear: people who go to hell choose to do so." Discuss.

4. What are some of the ways the Bible describes heaven? What do you think heaven will be like?

5. Have you made your final destiny secure? Do you know without a shadow of a doubt where you will spend eternity?

10

When Temptation Meets Endurance

The old cliché "between a rock and a hard place" took on new and frightful meaning when Aron Ralston's arm was trapped between a fallen boulder and a rock wall in the Bluejohn Canyon of Utah in April 2003.

The young backpacker called for help but knew he would not be heard. He had been hiking alone, and no one knew his exact location. Ralston had a small knife, but it was useless in chipping away rock.

For 127 hours he sipped the last of his water and tried to think of a way out of his dilemma. He concluded that there was only one way to escape with his life, and it was a slim chance. To free himself he would need to amputate his lower arm.

His knife was so dull that at first he could not even break the skin as he tried cutting himself. But a larger problem loomed. How would he ever cut through the bone? He had been trapped helplessly for five days and nights, and knew his mind and body were weakening badly.

Ralston took a deep breath and bent his arm against the rock so hard that the bone snapped. Then he gritted his teeth and cut through the flesh, freeing himself. He applied a crude tourniquet, wrapping the stump of his arm and willing himself to push through shock. His struggle wasn't over. He climbed out of the slot canyon, rappelled down a sixty-five-foot cliff, and hiked several miles, stumbling toward his vehicle. He was finally discovered by a family who called for emergency help. The amazing young man took the only way of escape that presented itself, grim as it was, and he survived.

It is a story that bears thinking about when we look at the amazing promise of God's Word. When we face temptation, there is always a way of escape. Even if we are caught between the rock and the hard place of circumstances and personal weakness up against the onslaught of the tempter, there is a way of escape.

First Corinthians 10:13 tells us this amazing truth: "No temptation has overtaken you except such as is common to man; but God is faithful, who will not allow you to be tempted beyond what you are able, but with the temptation will also make the way of escape, that you may be able to bear it."

Sometimes our way of escape may look grim and we think we can't possibly go there. But the joy of freedom turns out to be worth it. Usually our way of escape is much simpler than what Ralston faced. It is as obvious as booting down the computer or switching off the television, as easy as walking out the door of a place where we should not be, as basic as keeping our mouth shut or just saying no. But temptation is a force we must never trivialize. Temptation to sin requires superhuman strength to resist successfully.

We are going to look at the power of temptation in this chapter and at the drama that unfolded in a Judean wilderness, a place much like the wilderness of the Bluejohn Canyon of Utah, as Jesus faced down the tempter and found the way of escape. It is part of the modeling He did for us during His 1,000-day ministry, showing us how to live.

The entire story is told by both Matthew and Luke while Mark refers to it briefly. We'll look at Matthew's account, at the parallel temptation of Adam and Eve, and at the parallel temptation patterns that we experience today.

Satan's Strategy in Temptation

Matthew 4:1 says, "Then Jesus was led up by the Spirit into the wilderness to be tempted by the devil."

Have you noticed that your greatest temptations come after your greatest triumphs? The first word in this passage is the little word *then*. You could almost translate it *next* because Matthew is stressing that these things happened in succession.

Just before the temptation Jesus had gone through the marvelous experience of baptism. The Holy Spirit had come down in the form of a dove, and the Father had spoken from heaven and said this was His beloved Son. What a triumph that was! But after the baptism came the battle. After the ecstasy came the agony. So often that's the case in our lives. We experience a strong victory—maybe we conquer a sin or find success in sharing our faith with a friend, or we experience blessings at a retreat, or a specific prayer is answered. But shortly after that mountaintop, temptation comes in like a flood.

We need to understand that temptation itself is not sin. Temptation is the devil peeking through the keyhole of your heart into the room of your life. Sin is when you open the door and invite the devil in. It has been said that we can't stop the birds of temptation from flying over our heads, but we don't have to let them build nests in our hair. That is where the promise of 1 Corinthians 10:13 comes in. We can know the battle is never going to be stronger than we can bear. The temptations we face may get fierce, but the strength that God supplies is always greater, always waiting there for us to grab hold of. Whether the temptation is to an old familiar sin or to a new one taking us by surprise, there is always an exit strategy.

It is heartening to realize that Satan doesn't have any new tricks in his temptation arsenal. He has been using the same strategies since day one. Second Corinthians 2:11 tells us not to be ignorant of his methods. Satan always seems to come at us in one of three or a combination of three ways: physical, mental/emotional, or spiritual.

In the garden of Eden the devil came to Eve in just those ways. Genesis 3:6 tells us, "So when the woman saw that the tree was good for food [that was the appeal of the physical luring her along], that it was pleasant to the eyes [that was the appeal of the emotional], and a tree desirable to make one wise [that was the appeal of spiritual forces]." With all that, she gave in and ate the fruit.

A passage in 1 John 2:16 sounds strangely like the Genesis story: "For all that is in the world—the lust of the flesh [that's the physical], the lust of the eyes [that's emotional], and the pride of life [that's a spiritual appeal]—is not of the Father but is of the world."

The same way the devil tempted Eve is the same way he tempts you and me. The devil has only three moves on the chessboard of life, only three measly approaches to the human soul. But really, why should he change? He has been pretty successful with these three moves down through the centuries. But when he tried the same tricks on Jesus, Satan was in for a surprise.

Jesus is sometimes called the Last Adam, in contrast to the first Adam, the first man who ever lived. Let's compare the temptations of the two Adams and examine what happened as a result:

1. The first Adam was tempted in a garden, yielded, and turned the garden into a wilderness. Jesus was tempted in a wilderness, triumphed, and turned it into a garden.
2. The first Adam was tempted, fell, and ruined the human race. Jesus was tempted, won, and redeemed the human race.
3. The first Adam was tempted and collapsed. Jesus was tempted and conquered.

It's pretty clear that the story of Jesus' temptation is where we can learn how to win our own battles with temptation.

God's Purposes in Allowing Temptation

Maybe it surprises you that Matthew says Jesus was led by the Spirit into His temptation. That would be the Holy Spirit, part of the Trinity. Mark says that the Spirit actually drove Jesus into the wilderness. Clearly, God was behind this. God always has a purpose, a plan. In the case of this experience in the earthly life of His Son, God's plan was to exalt Jesus by showing His absolute sinlessness.

The late Dr. J. Vernon McGee of *Thru the Bible* radio ministry told a story that came from his boyhood in West Texas, a sparsely populated area in those days. The Santa Fe Railroad came through his little town and crossed the left fork of the Brazos River. In the summertime, McGee said, "There wasn't enough water in that river to rust a single nail, but in wintertime you could float a battleship on it."

One winter the river flooded high enough to wash out the Santa Fe Bridge, and the little town was without a train for a long time. Finally a new bridge was built, and the big day came. Two heavy engines were brought in and stopped on the bridge with their whistles tied down for effect. "Believe me, that was more whistling than we had ever heard in our little town! All twenty-three of us ran down to see what was happening," said McGee.

Someone asked the engineer in charge what they were doing, and the engineer replied, "Testing the bridge." The citizen asked, "Are you trying to break the bridge down?" The engineer laughed and almost sneered, saying, "Of course not. We're testing it to prove that it can't be broken down."[1]

That is exactly what was happening when Jesus faced temptation. God allowed the situation to prove that Jesus could not be broken down. When Satan came to meet Jesus in the wilderness that day, what the devil intended as a temptation to sin, the Father intended as a test to show the sinless perfection of His Son, Jesus.

Another purpose of the Father was to expose the devil. In Matthew 4:1, the devil is called *Diabolos*, which actually means "to throw through." He is the one who throws through the accusations at us. In Matthew 4:10 he is referred to as the *adversary*, the one who opposes us thoroughly. The names expose Satan for who he really is and what he is really like. The Bible teaches that Satan is very real. He is not a figment of imagination. Scripture describes him as a liar and a murderer. In this temptation experience Jesus talks to him in real conversation. Jesus is not having hallucinations; He is talking to a real, personal being. This passage demonstrates Satan's reality.

God has one more purpose in allowing this temptation of His beloved Son: to encourage you and me—because Jesus met temptation as a human and conquered it as a human. We now know Satan can be defeated by using the tools of victory. Hebrews 2:18 tells us, "For in that He Himself has suffered, being tempted, He is able to aid those who are tempted." He is able to rescue us.

The Core of Temptation

Let's read through this brief story and then take it apart and see how it applies to our lives:

> Now when the tempter came to Him, he said, "If You are the Son of God, command that these stones become bread." But He answered and said, "It is written, 'Man shall not live by bread alone, but by every word that proceeds from the mouth of God.'"
>
> Then the devil took Him up into the holy city, set Him on the pinnacle of the temple, and said to Him, "If You are the Son of God, throw Yourself down. For it is written: 'He shall give His angels charge over you,' and, 'In their hands they shall bear you up, lest you dash your foot against a stone.'" Jesus said to him, "It is written again, 'You shall not tempt the LORD your God.'"
>
> Again the devil took Him up on an exceedingly high mountain, and showed Him all the kingdoms of the world and their glory. And he said to Him, "All these thing I will give You if You will fall down and worship me." Then Jesus said to him, "Away with you, Satan! For it is written, 'You shall worship the LORD your God, and Him only you shall serve.'"
>
> Then the devil left Him, and behold, angels came and ministered to Him. (Matt. 4:3–11)

This was probably not the first time Jesus had been tempted, and it certainly was not the last. Satan would be back in fury in the Garden of Gethsemane and at the cross, and he'll be back in the future at the Battle of Armageddon. He was also likely active during the young life of Jesus, tempting Him even then. As a boy maybe Jesus was taunted by a school bully. Every school has one. Maybe at home He was tempted to retaliate against some jealous brother. Maybe over at the synagogue, where Jesus attended faithfully, He was tempted by a legalistic rabbi who wanted to turn life into a drab desert. Maybe at the town bazaar Jesus was tempted by the manipulations of a dishonest merchant.

But now it's a forty-day marathon temptation; Luke gives us the length (4:2). Probably there were running skirmishes between Jesus and the devil during those forty days in the wilderness when Jesus was fasting. But then they came to a head-on collision.

Don't get the idea that this was a piece of cake for Jesus just because He is God. He met this temptation, these wiles of the devil, with tools that are available to us. Ephesians 6:11 refers to the devil's wiles, a word that means "systematic temptations" or scientifically skillful temptations. They are so skillful and systematic that we are told to put on God's whole armor so we can withstand the evil day (v. 13). It may not hit us as hard as it hit Jesus, for He is the infinite one, but our evil days do come. Sometimes they hit unexpectedly, at a point we never dreamed that we would be hit. And Satan hits us with that triple whammy: physical, emotional/mental, and spiritual temptation.

Let's take a closer look at the three specific temptations Jesus faced. These are at the core of the same temptations we face today.

TEMPTATION #1: GIVE THE *NOW* PRIORITY OVER ETERNITY

This is essentially the physical aspect of temptation—gotta eat, gotta breathe, gotta have sex, gotta grab material things, and gotta grab them now. The old snake came to Jesus when the Lord was hungry and thirsty and said, "If." Greek scholars call that a first-class conditional introduction to a sentence. It assumes that the first part of the sentence is true; therefore, the second part is true. The devil makes an assumption. It could be translated, "Since You are the Son of God, then command that these stones become bread." Or "Since You are who You are, and You've got to be hungry, go on, make some bread. What's stopping You?"

It had been forty days and forty nights since Jesus had eaten. You bet He was hungry. He lived His life in a normal body with normal human appetites. Of course Jesus could have turned those stones into bread. He would later multiply a few loaves and fish to feed thousands. He would take water and turn it into wine. Turn stones into bread? No problem.

That's exactly how Satan tempts us today. He appeals to our normal physical needs and appetites. We may argue that God has given us these desires; therefore, it is only normal to satisfy them. Satan will push that argument. That kind of reasoning is behind the temptation to take illegal drugs, consume excessive alcohol, and engage in illicit sexual activity. God made you that way, Satan insists, so you have no choice but to give in and fulfill those desires.

Jesus' answer to Satan's argument may surprise you. It may not sound like much of a defense at first. He refers to some words that were written long ago. Jesus said, "It is written," using the perfect tense verb that means "it was written, it stands written, it will continue and be abidingly written." Then Jesus told Satan exactly what is written to refute this temptation: "Man shall not live by bread alone" (Deut. 8:3).

Jesus didn't say that man shall not live by bread. That would be incorrect. You must have bread; you must have physical needs met. Jesus told us another time that our Father knows we need physical things. But to the devil He stressed that humans shall not live by bread *alone*. He was saying the physical is not the main thing in life. Immediate needs are not nearly as important as eternal needs.

Notice Jesus used the word *man*, meaning all humans. He was telling the devil He is a human, not an animal. Satan argues that our normal physical desires are no different from animal instincts. It is true that you can choose to live on the level of barnyard animals; many people do. But you are not just a higher form of animal. You are human. You are made in the image of God. Satan argues that we should fulfill normal physical desires in abnormal ways.

TEMPTATION #2: TRUST IN A DIFFERENT PLAN THAN GOD'S PLAN

Satan had a second trick up his sleeve. Okay, he didn't succeed in getting Jesus to turn stones into bread, but he will face off with Jesus in the emotional/mental arena. He will try to detour Jesus to a different plan.

He took Jesus to Jerusalem, possibly by a vision, and set Him on a pinnacle or wing of the temple. Some scholars believe that referred to the flat-topped roof on Solomon's porch. Wherever it was exactly, it was evidently the highest place on the temple. Down below was the Brook Kidron, an estimated 450-foot drop. People down there would look like ants. The temptation consisted of simply trying to persuade Jesus to jump. Have you noticed the devil can persuade but can't push? A comic named Flip Wilson became famous by insisting the devil made him do it, whenever he did anything foolish. The truth is that the devil can't make you do anything you are not willing to do.

Satan was more subtle than last time—he walked up to Jesus with a Bible under his arm. He can quote scripture too, and referred to Psalm 91:11–12. Actually he mangled it, took it out of context, and dropped some of it, mutilating the scripture for his purposes. He twisted scripture to tell Jesus that angels would catch Him if He jumped. He inferred that Jesus would be a sensation if He pulled off this stunt. The trick Satan used was to appeal to the human need for acceptance, basically saying to Jesus, "Listen, You're not getting anywhere. You're thirty years old and You're a nobody. Do something spectacular, and You'll be accepted." Satan knows we all want acceptance.

Jesus answered, "It is written," and quoted from Deuteronomy 6:16, "You shall not tempt the LORD your God." Oh, He certainly could have done it. He could have floated down with an angel escort. The crowd would have gasped and applauded. He could have called a press conference. But He chose to model that it's not necessary to go to extremes to be accepted, that we don't need to go outside God's plan. He chose not to give in to the emotional appeal. And we don't have to either. Acceptance is never worth the price of poor behavioral choices. We can always say no.

TEMPTATION #3: TAKE THE EASY ROUTE TO SUCCESS

Next, Satan took Jesus to a high mountain. The devil doesn't need to take most of us to a very high mountain to get us to sin; just some little low thing will usually get us. Maybe it's the temptation to cheat on your tax return, pad your expense account, view a pornographic website, listen to a tasty bit of gossip, or give in to a grouchy fit of temper.

But Satan knew he needed to take Jesus to the heights of temptation. This was the ultimate spiritual temptation. Satan was trying to get Jesus to skip the cross. He was saying, "Why should You suffer and die to be Lord of all when I can give it to You on a silver platter?" So they went to a high mountain, and Satan displayed all the kingdoms of the world and their glories. He offered it all to Jesus for a moment of devil-worship. Somehow Satan showed it all in a few moments, perhaps through a vision. Jesus viewed Rome with its military splendor. He saw the cultural brilliance of Greece. He saw China's exotic treasures. He looked backward and forward in time and saw the might of the British Empire, the Nazi regime, the Soviet Union, the United States, and more. And Satan said, "Jesus, You can have it all."

Could he have given it? Yes, he's the prince of this world. Would he have given it? No. The devil never delivers what he promises. He promises the next affair will satisfy. He promises just one more drink will do the job. He promises just a little more money will fulfill you. All lies.

Basically Satan urged Jesus to do this thing just once, and do it now. To paraphrase, he said, "Jesus, just bend the knee one time. That's all You need to do. Worship me just once." That is one of the devil's big lies: "Try this just once; if you don't like it, no big deal."

Jesus answered brilliantly. He told Satan to get lost and reminded him again that something powerful had been written. He quoted Deuteronomy 6:13: "You shall worship the LORD your God, and Him only you shall serve." God alone is tops and worthy of worship, and what you worship, that is what you serve.

How We Can Meet Temptation

It's encouraging to know that we have this same ammunition to use against Satan that Jesus used, the same weapons that caused the devil to leave after this three-pronged attack. Angels came and ministered to Jesus, probably cooked Him a meal. We can have the same experience of victory in the temptations we face. Here are the three keys:

1. Remember that Jesus is present. When you are tempted, keep in mind that Jesus is living in you, and "He who is in you is greater than he who is in the world" (1 John 4:4).
2. Remember that Jesus met His temptation in the power of the Holy Spirit. That same Holy Spirit is available to you and me. Ephesians 5:18 tells us to "be filled with the Spirit." We can yield our lives daily to the fullness, the control, of the Spirit, allowing Him to do what He came inside us to do.
3. Remember to use the ammunition that Satan can't handle: Scripture. You have the Word of God. Fill your mind and heart with God's Word. Psalm 119:11 tells us to hide God's Word in our hearts so that we won't sin against Him, so we can resist temptation.

But what if it's too late? Maybe as you read these words, you are aware that you have fallen big time into some temptation. One of Satan's big lies is that if you have fallen, you belong to him. He says things such as, "You've done it now. I've got you. You're hooked. There's no hope for you." But the truth is, that is just not so. Failure is not final. Hope is found in the same wonderful written Word of God. Take all the messed-up places of your life to 1 John 1:9: "If we confess our sins, He is faithful and just to forgive us our sins and to cleanse us from all unrighteousness." You don't have to live in that sin.

Picture that victory scene in the Judean wilderness when Jesus and Satan squared off. The devil hits his first blow, the strongest physical temptation possible, and Jesus picks up the sword of the Spirit, the Word of God. Slash! The devil rolls away battered. A second time Satan tries, offering the ultimate emotional-mental temptation, and Jesus uses the sword again. Swish! Satan stumbles, bruised and bleeding. A third time Satan lashes out, this time with the zenith of spiritual temptation. Jesus wields the sword of the Word. Stab! And Satan crumbles, beaten.

Jesus is the victor. And He's on our side.

That same victory against temptation can be ours too.

Sometimes our way to escape may look grim and we think we can't possibly resist temptation. But the joy of freedom turns out to be worth it.

QUESTIONS FOR INDIVIDUAL REFLECTION
OR SMALL GROUP DISCUSSION

1. Let's make this section very practical. What are some of the biggest temptations facing you, and what's your typical pattern of response?
2. When you give in to temptation, how do you feel afterward? Conversely, when you resist temptation, how do you feel afterward?
3. According to this chapter, why do you think God had Jesus face temptation? What did facing temptation show about Jesus?
4. What three temptations did the devil bring to Jesus, and how are those temptations similar to what we face today?
5. What three methods of resisting temptation does Jonathan outline at the end of the chapter?

11

Beyond the Hype

Each year when the Super Bowl is played, security forces pay special attention. The United States Homeland Security Department ranks it as a Level One security event, and that designation kicks loose millions in federal funds to put in place extra law enforcement and technical support, sophisticated surveillance equipment, and the latest crowd monitoring devices. Air space is restricted and policed by the North American Aerospace Defense Command. The massive annual security effort that goes along with being host for the Super Bowl includes low-flying government planes, bomb-sniffing dogs, magnetometers, high-tech mobile robots, and FBI agents who are trained to handle shooters, bombs, and even nuclear threats.

Leading up to the 2011 Super Bowl in Dallas, NBC News reported that U.S. counterterrorism and law enforcement officials studied the situation and reported there were no credible terrorist threats surrounding the game, but its high profile could make it a desirable target. One reason this Super Bowl got extra attention is that former President George W. Bush and his wife, Laura, attended. The NFL's own security division spent about $6 million on making the game safe.

Dial backward about twenty centuries, and we see another situation that officials of the day perceived as a security threat. In Jerusalem, Israel, an event took place that could have stirred up trouble, and officials brought in the Roman guard (called the *Praetorian Guard*), just to be there to make sure nothing would get out of control and no one would cause problems.

It happened near the end of Jesus' 1,000-day ministry. He had taught, healed, performed miracles, lived an exemplary life before His disciples, and now it was coming to a climax. This event with the high security risk is usually called the triumphal entry, and it marks the beginning of the end of Jesus' earthly ministry. It began near Jerusalem on the Mount of Olives, overlooking the city across the Kidron Valley. Nearby were places that would later be filled with the drama of Jesus' final week. There was the Garden of Gethsemane where Jesus will agonize in prayer and where they will arrest Him. There was the Antonia Fortress where they will mock Him, beat Him, and put the crown of thorns on His head. There was Golgotha, Calvary, just outside the city gate where they will crucify Him. And there was a tomb, from which He will walk out, alive. But a week before all that, Jesus went through the experience of the triumphal entry.

About to begin His entry from the vantage point of the Mount of Olives, Jesus looked over the whole of the beautiful city of Jerusalem. Prophetically He looked into the heart of the city and saw the externalism of its religious life and it broke His heart.

The story raises for us an important issue today. Will we follow Jesus no matter what? Will we be able to look beyond the hype that often accompanies religiosity to where we find the real person of Jesus? And will He be enough for us?

EVERYONE IS AT RISK

In this ancient security situation, anyone could have been a terrorist or troublemaker, so everyone was being watched by someone. Everyone was at risk, just as today in our spiritual lives, we are all at risk of destruction from the enemy of our souls. We never know exactly where the attack may come from. As we discussed in the previous chapter, attacks and temptations may be physical, mental, emotional, or spiritual. An attack can come from within or without, from the world, the flesh, or the devil. We have to be constantly on guard. Let's see how people handled it that day.

This was Passover Week, one of the biggest celebrations on the Jewish calendar. There were three feasts during the year called pilgrimage feasts, when Jews were supposed to go to Jerusalem. First, there was Passover, also called the Feast of Unleavened Bread; second, the Feast of Tabernacles; and third, the Feast of Weeks, also called Pentecost. So on this day, thousands of people were pressing into Jerusalem for the Passover celebration. The marketplaces were bustling. Vendors hawked their wares in the streets, getting out into the milling crowds so they could do business and make as much money as possible. When you visit Israel today, you can walk through the old city, and it is much the same. The merchants know tourists are coming, so they are out there ready to do business. You can hardly take a step without a vendor trying to sell you something.

Back in that day the Romans who ruled Israel knew that all the crowds traveling into the city meant the possibility of unrest. Imagine that—unrest in the Middle East. Nothing new here. The Romans prepared by sending in the Praetorian Guard, stationing them at the Antonia Fortress. The fortress was built by Herod just behind the temple, in honor of his dear friend Antony, of the famous Roman duo Antony and Cleopatra. Today in Jerusalem you can see part of this fortress. Excavated on a lower level is the original courtyard of the Antonia Fortress, the place where these guards were stationed and where Jesus would later be beaten and mocked, spit upon and crowned with thorns. Hundreds of guards milled around, checked their armor, polished their weapons, played games to while away the time, possibly did training exercises, ready to apply the full force of the law if things got out of hand. Passover was always a testy time in the city. Emotions ran high, and the hype was fuelled by mob mentality. At the very least officials might expect a few riot situations.

During Passover week, religious leaders opened the doors of the temple. When Messiah came, descending from the Mount of Olives as they knew He was predicted to do, from the east toward the temple, the open doors symbolized that He was welcome.

But there were a couple of problems. One was that the religious establishment of the day did not really believe that Messiah would come that week or any time. Most didn't believe in a personal Messiah at all. Some who did had probably grown jaded because the nation had been waiting so long for Messiah and He hadn't shown up yet. But the leaders were going through the motions of saying they believed in Him and welcomed Him. They had all the symbols. They had all the right moves. The story is beginning to sound familiar, isn't it? Today we have people, sometimes leaders, sometimes Christians, who have all the right moves, all the symbols and ceremonies, but no reality in their dealing with Messiah. Maybe you sense at times that description applies to you. Possibly you have been going through the motions; perhaps you know how to speak Christianese, but God is not real to you. Stick with the story. There is a way out of that false world.

A second problem in that day was that opening the temple doors to welcome Messiah also provided opportunity for insurrectionists or false prophets to come and claim they were Messiah. They could gather a group of followers on the Mount of Olives, march down through the Kidron Valley, and come into the temple to try to overthrow Rome and establish their own rule. If it happened this particular Passover day, it would not be the first time someone had tried it. That is why the Praetorian Guards were ready. They would quell any riot, any insurrection, any hyped-up Messiah figure. They would stop it by doing that day's equivalent of rolling tanks down the streets and opening fire, killing them all, if necessary.

This was more than theoretical law enforcement. In Acts 5, Gamaliel speaks of two who were executed in just such situations. Theudas claimed to be somebody special, and four hundred followers rallied around him, but he was killed. Judas the Galilean led a band of people in revolt against Rome, but he was also killed and his followers scattered (vv. 34–37).

So into this tense political hotbed, Jesus made a significant move. His entry into the city, His presentation of Himself as Messiah, turned out to be a decision point for a lot of people. They had to face the question, "Will I follow Jesus no matter what?" It may sound like a familiar question because it is one we all have to face too.

EVERYBODY HAS SOMEBODY FOR A KING

Watch as the story unfolds, and picture yourself in the crowd that day. Which group of people do you identify with?

> And it came to pass, when He drew near to Bethphage and Bethany, at the mountain called Olivet, that He sent two of His disciples, saying, "Go into the village opposite you, where as you enter you will find a colt tied, on which no one has ever sat. Loose it and bring it here. And if anyone asks you, 'Why are you loosing it?' thus you shall say to him, 'Because the Lord has need of it.'" (Luke 19:29–31)

So the disciples obeyed, and it happened just as He had said it would. They brought the colt of a donkey to Jesus, threw their own coats on its back, and hoisted Jesus up. Right away, people began spreading coats on the road in front of Him, a gesture of respect and honor.

> Then, as He was now drawing near the descent of the Mount of Olives, the whole multitude of the disciples began to rejoice and praise God with a loud voice for all the mighty works they had seen, saying:
>
> "'Blessed is the King who comes in the name of the LORD!'
> Peace in heaven and glory in the highest!"
>
> And some of the Pharisees called to Him from the crowd, "Teacher, rebuke Your disciples."
> But He answered and said to them, "I tell you that if these should keep silent, the stones would immediately cry out." (Luke 19:37–40)

John gave us a little more information: as well as laying coats and cloaks on the road before Jesus, they were waving palm branches and at the same time, calling, "Hosanna! Blessed is He who comes in the name of the LORD! The King of Israel!" (John 12:13).

It was an incredible moment for each person in this crowd. Keep in mind the Praetorian Guard standing ready. Keep in mind the danger, the crowds, the tension, the possibility of security threats all around, and how easily a person could be swept up and charged with some crime just by being in the wrong place at the wrong time. Anything you did to draw attention to yourself could bring on trouble. Naturally speaking, people would not want to raise their voices.

But notice the little key word in Luke 19:37: *began*. Despite all the danger, people began to rejoice and praise God, and they did it loudly. Some probably had questionable motives, but some had made deep heart-decisions that, no matter how dangerous it was, they would raise their voices to praise God.

I was in Israel recently with a group of people, and we stood in this area taking pictures of the Mount of Olives. Nearby a tense situation arose. An Arab had sold his property to some Jewish people in an Arab community. Some of the Arab leaders have made laws against doing that. We observed a crowd of people out in the streets fighting, throwing rocks at each other. Since my camera was in my hands, I took hundreds of pictures. Suddenly things changed. We heard pops that sounded like fireworks and realized it was much more than that. Explosions of tear gas flew into the crowd. Israeli military personnel had showed up and were intent on stopping this riot and rock-throwing battle. And they did. This is the kind of thing that the Roman guards were expecting to break out back in the first century as Jesus rode down Mount Olivet.

Jesus began His slow journey on that little donkey, down the trail from the Mount of Olives, down toward the Brook Kidron in the valley. People gathered along the way, following, daring to raise their voices in praise, willing to run the risk that the guard would storm out of that Antonia Fortress swinging their swords and spears, not bothering to ask questions until later.

Maybe somebody whispered, "Remember what Zechariah said six hundred years ago?" "Rejoice greatly, O daughter of Zion! Shout, O daughter of Jerusalem! Behold, your King is coming to you; He is just and having salvation, lowly and riding on a donkey, a colt, the foal of a donkey" (Zech. 9:9). And maybe the buzz spread. They began to remember things Jesus had taught, and asked one another, "Could this be the one who will deliver us? Could this be our king?" They had probably talked about it around the campfires as they traveled to Jerusalem from various towns. Maybe this Jesus was the one who would deliver Israel from Roman domination, just as Moses had led the people out of slavery in Egypt. They knew the temple doors were open, and they desperately hoped Jesus would be the promised deliverer. They hoped He would head right in there and set up His kingdom.

REAL WORSHIP OR INDIVIDUAL AGENDAS

As Jesus rode along He had a full view of the temple mount. Today there is a mosque on that spot, but the temple stood there in His day. Jesus could ride through the eastern gates of the city and right into the temple courts. The people were so excited that He might actually do that, they risked their lives to shout His name, along with other taboos: "hosanna," "blessed," and "the king of Israel."

But a big problem emerged. Clearly the crowd was hoping this man on the donkey would give them a political and military victory, saving them from political oppression and the social and economic problems they were facing. The big problem was that they were not facing their spiritual needs, which was the main focus of His coming. There was a big disconnect between their expectations and Jesus' plan.

You get a clue in the words they used. John 12:13 tells us they cried out, "Hosanna," which means "save now," referring to saving from oppression. It was political terminology. They also used political symbols. Palm branches were more than just the handiest thing to pick up. They symbolized victory. I have a coin that dates from fifty to one hundred years before the time of Jesus. It is a Jewish coin with palm branches engraved on it. They used palm branches on coinage because it symbolized victory—military, political victory.

About 150 years before Jesus' time, Judas Maccabeus led the

Maccabean Revolt that delivered the Jewish people from oppression. The Jewish people of Jesus' day kept hoping it would happen again and last longer. So now with Jesus coming down the trail, this miracle worker, this one who fed multitudes and walked on water—if they hadn't seen these things themselves, you can be sure they'd heard about them—the place was going wild. Their hopes were up, way up. Hopes for deliverance from Roman oppression.

The Pharisees recognized what the people meant. They called to Jesus, saying, "*Teacher*, rebuke Your disciples" (Luke 19:39, emphasis added). The Pharisees heard the loud noise and understood the meaning. They were saying, "Please shut them up. Don't let them say that. They're going to bring the full force of Rome down on our heads. We're all going to die." They were suddenly afraid for their lives. Jesus' answer is amazing. He said that real praise can't be shut up. "He answered and said to them, 'I tell you that if these should keep silent, the stones would immediately cry out'" (Luke 19:40).

When I walked down that road in Israel recently, I stooped and picked up a stone. The road I walked on is only a couple of hundred years old. But down below a wall, the foundations are still there, and you can see parts of the original road. That's where I picked up a rock. I thought about the fact that this was the very road where Jesus had ridden, presenting His kingship to His people. This was where people threw down palm branches and coats and cloaks and cried out blessings to the name of the Lord. The road on which I walked was the place where the Pharisees turned on Him in fury and told Him to make them be quiet. And Jesus answered "If I do, the very rocks will cry out." I picked up one of those rocks to help me remember, to symbolize for me that our lives need to be shouting out, "Blessed is the King who comes in the name of the LORD" (Luke 19:38). We need to be praising Him, whatever the risk, whatever the cost.

As the crowd that day screamed, "Hosanna!" it was probably all about politics for most individuals although, for some, it may have been real worship. They all needed to learn that Jesus had a better plan than politics. Oh yes, His kingdom will be set up on this earth someday. But Jesus said, "No, this is not the time." He looked at

Jerusalem with tears in His eyes because He knew what was to come. He knew that in a few short days, He would lay down His life to give us the ultimate gift. Way beyond political or social deliverance of any kind, He would give us spiritual deliverance. Way beyond peace between nations, He would give us salvation that would provide eternal peace for our souls.

BEING REAL WITH GOD

It is salvation and a deep appreciation for it that rouses in our hearts expressions of true worship. When we come to grips with what Jesus has done for us in His death, burial, and resurrection, we can't help but cry out in praise to Him, regardless of risk, regardless of cost. We will follow Him no matter what.

That day as the crowd screamed, "Hosanna!" calling for political deliverance, and the Pharisees screamed in fury, "Stop them!" in fear for their lives, Jesus would offer a better way. As Jesus moved closer to the city, He stopped at a vantage point and began to weep. He said, "If you had known, even you, especially in this your day, the things that make for your peace!" (Luke 19:42). But they didn't know they refused their King; they refused their Savior, and Jesus foresaw that the city would be destroyed. The prophecy He spoke that day, looking up at the temple mount, came true in AD 70, when Roman legions swept in under General Titus and destroyed the city, leveling the temple. Today, two thousand years later, that temple is still destroyed, with not one stone upon another, just as Jesus said would happen.

In the midst of a pep rally, an event full of celebration, with people crying out praises to Him, Jesus stopped with tears in His eyes. He looked at the city and saw something different than what everyone else saw. He saw the proud city and knew it would be destroyed. He saw the people making those statements of worship and knew that deep down it wasn't real for most of them. Oh, maybe there were individuals who truly worshipped Him with all their hearts and received Him as Savior and Lord, but for the crowds it was mainly hype. How do we know this? A few days later, many of these same people will cry out, "Crucify Him! Crucify Him!" They will reject Him. The religious leaders, of course, had already rejected Him and were seeking a way to turn Him over to the Romans for crucifixion.

The first triumphal entry of Jesus ended at the cross. A few days later the praising crowd turned ugly and demanded His execution. Jesus will come a second time to this earth, and Zechariah 14 tells us His feet will again stand on the Mount of Olives, and He will ride through the gates of Jerusalem. This time He will enter Jerusalem in triumph, and from there He will rule the world.

Today the questions for us are simple but searching:

1. When Jesus looks at me, are there tears in His eyes? Does He see a person voicing praises to Him, but without authenticity? In joining the singing at church services, is my heart in it? Do I sense true worship rising within me when I listen to others praise Him? Can I look beyond hype and entertainment—even Christian entertainment—and find the reverence of a spirit of true worship? Do I know how to worship Him in spirit and in truth? Can I get beyond the hype of a superficial experience to genuine worship?

2. When Jesus looks at me, is He weeping over me? Maybe He is telling me what He said to the city of Jerusalem that day: "You, even you, if you would understand the elements of peace with God, you could claim it. Yes, even you." Can I get beyond the mob hype to find real relationship with Him?

3. When Jesus looks at me, is He seeing a modern-day Pharisee? Is there a deep fury within me against His kingship? Maybe I am holding back part of my life or the whole of my life from His rule. Am I telling Him I will not have Him to rule over me?

4. When Jesus looks at me, does He see a person focused on the wrong things? Am I occupied with social revolution, political solutions, economic ideas, psychological methods, or material things instead of resting my hopes in true spiritual deliverance? God often uses these things, but the heart of our deliverance

is spiritual because the heart of our need is spiritual. Can I get beyond the hype of my agenda to find His plan?

5. When Jesus looks at me, does He see a person locked in fear? Jesus wants followers who will risk it all—living expressions of praise to Him—no matter who hears or who sees. Can I face the risks? Perhaps it's risk of reputation, or risk of losing a relationship. In some places today, it's risk of losing life itself. Can I face the risks and pledge that I will follow Jesus no matter what?

6. Maybe when Jesus looks at me, He sees a little bit of all these persons. I need to ask Him to help me identify my needs and claim the solutions that come from His heart. May His weeping over me turn to tears of joy.

For each one of these groups and individuals beside the road heading into Jerusalem that day, as for each one of us, the important truth is that nowhere is authenticity more important than when it comes to worship. Worship is rendering the whole of life to Him, and doing so in bottom-line reality, in spirit and in truth.

Ruth Bell Graham, the wife of Dr. Billy Graham, once shared that early in her married life when the cares of a young family and household pressed heavily, she did not like the chore of washing dishes. To help keep the task in perspective, she posted a sign over the kitchen sink that read, "Divine service is performed here three times daily."

May we lead similar lives of sincerity, purpose, and true devotion to God.

QUESTIONS FOR INDIVIDUAL REFLECTION
OR SMALL GROUP DISCUSSION

1. People follow Jesus for a lot of different reasons. Some of these reasons may be true to His purpose and some not. What are some of the reasons people follow Jesus, and what are some things people hope to get from Him?

2. When people follow Jesus for the wrong reasons, what usually results?

3. In what manner did Jesus enter Jerusalem? Why did Jesus enter the way He did?

4. What do you think some of the people were hoping for as they welcomed Jesus into the city?

5. What are some valid reasons to follow Jesus?

12

PEACE—NOW

A young man, moving along in life, realized he was doing well. He had a wonderful wife whom he deeply loved, two delightful children, a good job, and a comfortable home. He loved and believed in God and took his family to a good church regularly. He was living the Christian American dream, right?

But suddenly the bottom fell out. His wife was diagnosed with inoperable cancer. Shock, disbelief, tears, turmoil—you can imagine what they went through. As weeks went on, the man was troubled by nightmares, and each morning when he woke up, he realized the nightmare was real life. "It was as if all the ground under me was crumbling away like sand," he said.

He prayed; he begged God; he got Christian friends to pray; he consulted with doctors; he read all the information he could get his hands on. "I prayed like a grown-up, and I prayed like a little kid, just, 'Please-please-please, dear God, please don't let her die,'" he said. He poured out his need to God: "I can't do this. I can't raise these kids on my own."

Nothing changed in her situation. His response was continued panic. He lost weight, couldn't eat, couldn't sleep, couldn't concentrate. He felt he was losing his mind and feared he would become a burden instead of a caregiver to his wife.

One day the panic slammed him while he was driving, causing him to pull over. There by the side of the road, sobs engulfed him. As he told it later, "Suddenly it was as if a hand was laid on my shoulder, and God said, *It's going to be all right*."

His wife was not miraculously healed, but treatment began, and she found a path of gratitude and determination to live each day fully, however many days were allotted to her. The man's panic subsided, and he began to meet the ongoing crisis with maturity and resources he didn't know he had. The future is still uncertain, but supernatural peace is their daily experience.

Have you ever found yourself in a similar situation? Undoubtedly your time of great need looks different than this young man's. But have you ever found yourself in times of huge distress, pressure, stress, and perhaps even panic?

Toward the end of Jesus' 1,000-day ministry, the disciples found themselves in the midst of dire circumstances. So Jesus laid His hand on their shoulders as they confronted their greatest trial, told them, "It's going to be all right," and gave them peace. That's the amazing story we'll look at in this chapter. Possibly no story in the New Testament is more helpful to us when we are going through times of turmoil and in need of God's peace.

ALONE, IN DANGER, IN PANIC

After the hype of the triumphal entry experience that we looked at in the last chapter, Jesus pulled His disciples aside and took them to an upper room for a quiet interlude. He knew that His time with them was short (although they did not). He will soon go through horrendous suffering and death. They will feel confused, alone, and abandoned; their own lives will be in danger; they will experience all the pressures that cause utter panic. At this point Jesus pulled away from the active ministry He had been doing for nearly 1,000 days, to spend intimate time with His disciples. He probably reasoned that people had seen all of His power that they needed. He had healed people. He had raised the dead. He had taught great truths of heaven to people on earth. Now it was time to gather His twelve special friends to spend some private time preparing them for what would take place.

Research tells us that number one on the stress meter is the experience of losing a loved one. The disciples will go through this; and more than a loved one, they will lose the one they expected to set up a kingdom, the one to whom they had committed their lives and careers. They will feel, in the confusion after His death, that they had lost their faith, their reason for living. We know the end of the story, we know about the resurrection, but they did not. They will feel completely alone, without their best friend, without a Savior, without a reason to go on. They may even feel angry, suspecting that they had been duped. Jesus knew that what they were about to face would be the most difficult time of their lives, and He will not be there in bodily form to help them. He wanted to give them some last instructions. The setting was a dinner that Jesus and His disciples shared, in a borrowed upper room. The story is told in John 13.

As the dinner ended, Jesus washed the disciples' feet. He was the King of kings, the Lord of lords, the Son of God, but He knelt before them and did this humble task. Some protested, but Jesus said that He needed to do this because He came to serve rather than be served. Jesus did this willingly to model for us how to serve one another.

As the evening continued, Jesus identified the person who would betray Him. These twelve men had followed and ministered with Him day by day, but He knew one would betray Him. When Jesus told them this fact, they were shocked. John was sitting beside Jesus, and Peter motioned to John, "Go on, ask Him." So John asked Jesus pointedly who He was talking about. Jesus told John that it was Judas Iscariot, and at that moment Judas slipped out, and the Bible says that Satan actually entered him (v. 27). That's what it takes to do such a vile deed. Besides Jesus, only John knew who it was, and he was likely too stunned to do anything. The others, if they noticed, probably thought Judas was heading out to buy some supplies he had forgotten because he was in charge of the checkbook.

Their attention turned to another shocking thing that Jesus was saying. He said one of the Twelve would deny Him. Someone would deny that he even knew who Jesus was. Can you imagine the scene? These men had walked away from everything to follow Jesus. They knew what it had cost them to take up the life of discipleship, and now they had to grapple with the announcement that one of them would deny Him. The room must have been in turmoil as they coped with shock and disbelief. At this point a storm was brewing in that room, and Jesus knew He needed to calm things down.

If you are part of a family, you know that moments like this come. Recently the six of us in our family were gathered at a meal and things began to escalate. People began talking louder and louder, and some food began to fly across the room. In a situation like that, somebody has to just say, "Stop! Let's all calm down now." It's kind of like a reboot.

In a far more serious scene, that is what Jesus did in the Upper Room that night when things began to escalate. He knew, with what they were facing, they needed peace.

REBOOTING FOR PEACE

Every one of us gets into situations of turmoil when we feel confused and helpless. It feels as though everything is out of control, we don't know what to do, and maybe we are losing our grip. You might be in that kind of turmoil right now as you read these words. The turmoil could be caused by circumstances that seem over the top, or by inner struggles, by relationships that turned upside down, by finances that went sideways, by hurts and betrayals. In times like these, we desperately need peace—peace that goes way beyond the natural.

A few chapters back we looked at the story of Jesus out on the Sea of Galilee with His disciples when a deadly storm came up. Remember what He did? Mark 4:39 says, "Then He arose and rebuked the wind, and said to the sea, 'Peace, be still!' And the wind ceased and there was a great calm." That's the kind of peace we long to have spoken into our storms, isn't it?

As Jesus continued teaching the eleven remaining disciples in the Upper Room, He clearly told them that He was going away but gave several reasons why they didn't need to be troubled about it. Throughout His conversation that evening, Jesus communicated the idea of personal peace. In John 14:27, spoken during that evening gathering, Jesus said, "Peace I leave with you. My peace I give to you; not as the world gives do I give to you. Let not your heart be troubled, neither let it be afraid."

Even in the way Jesus shaped that promise, people in the first century would get the emphasis. In the original language of that day, the first word of a sentence was the most important. You and I, if we had spoken this statement, may have said, "I leave peace with you. I'm going to give you peace." If I were going to give you food, I wouldn't say, "Food I give to you." If I intended to give you a dollar bill, I wouldn't say, "Dollar bill I give to you." Today in the way we use our language, we would say, "Hey, I'm going to give you a dollar." But Jesus structured the sentence this way so they would understand that the most important thing He had to say was, "Peace."

There is another important word to notice: "Leave." You don't leave something behind if you are staying. Yes, Jesus was leaving soon. He set the stage for the fact that He would soon be gone, and they would no longer see Him every day. He was leaving them peace because He was, in fact, leaving.

At the beginning of John 14, Jesus expanded on why He was leaving, where He was going, and what He'll be doing: "Let not your heart be troubled; you believe in God, believe also in Me. In My Father's house are many mansions; if it were not so, I would have told you. I go to prepare a place for you. And if I go and prepare a place for you, I will come again and receive you to Myself; that where I am, there you may be also" (vv. 1–3).

Jesus said this to calm their turmoil. These were frightened children; the shadow of the cross had fallen on this little group. There in the Upper Room as they faced the difficult future, He wanted them to understand the depths of peace. They had seen Jesus as a person of power. He had healed the sick, stilled the storm, and raised the dead. Now the One with all this power was about to be shackled, beaten, and nailed to a cross. Jesus wanted to make sure they understood that He could calm and comfort them in the midst of all this and that it was going to be all right.

Let's look a little closer at why He can make that promise.

COMPASSION OF THE PEACE GIVER

Jesus was not mouthing empty words. He showed His disciples that His own compassion is at the heart of the peace we seek. We can always trust Jesus to be compassionate. He told them—and you can almost hear the compassion in His voice—"Let not your heart be troubled" (John 14:1). The word *troubled* is *tarasso* in the original language. It means "extreme turmoil." That same word was used in John 5 in the story of the man at the Pool of Bethesda who wanted to get into the healing water when it was troubled, that is, when it was stirred or agitated. This isn't a simple word that means things are not going so well, but it's a word for extreme turmoil. It is used when things are rocky, when circumstances are just about as rough as life can dish out. The word was also used in Matthew 2 to describe Herod's anger when he was told the Messiah had been born. When he learned a king of the Jews had been born, Herod's response was to try to kill all the male children two years old or younger and hope that this maniacal dragnet would get rid of this king. He was *troubled* by what he had heard; he was in *extreme turmoil*. The word was used again in John 11 when Jesus stood at the tomb of Lazarus, His friend who had died. In describing Jesus' feelings that day, the writer says that He groaned in His spirit and was troubled. He was in *extreme turmoil*.

When Jesus told His friends in the Upper Room not to let their hearts be troubled, He used that word for a good reason. He wanted them to understand that He knew their hearts would be rocked by severe turmoil, and that they were going to be agitated in spirit to unbelievable lengths by events that would unfold. He wanted them to see they could experience peace in the midst of the most horrific event that would ever take place in the history of the world. You and I are not in that extreme situation, but we are often locked into some kind of turmoil, some kind of situation that feels completely out of control. To us, Jesus also speaks His promise of peace. And He tells us from His heart of compassion that He understands.

CREDIBILITY OF THE PEACE SPEAKER

Did you notice that Jesus, the compassionate peace giver, urged us in that passage to believe? But it's not a belief in some fairy tale that makes the difference. It is believing in the Father and the Son. "You believe in God, believe also in Me" (John 14:1). Here's the thing: we can believe in Him because He is credible.

What a difference it makes if the person who speaks peace to us, the person who tells us everything's going to be all right, is a credible person, someone we trust completely. When my daughter Jessica was about eighteen months old, I was at home with the two little ones while my wife, Shari, was out of town on a ministry event. One night I was watching TV as the kids were running around. I was trying to tune them out because, you know, that's what dads do.

Suddenly I heard this horrific scream. I mean a blood-curdling scream, the kind you hear in horror movies. I jumped up and ran to the kitchen, the source of the scream, and there I found Jessica in a state of extreme turmoil that got me into a state of extreme turmoil too. She was lying on the kitchen floor facedown. She had fallen somehow and had hit her head on the corner of a wall and cut her head open. Today she has a cute little scar as a reminder of the accident, but that day, she was lying facedown, bleeding, and I was scared to death.

My first thought was—being honest here—*What's Shari going to do to me?* But I quickly rolled Jessica over and wrapped my arms around her. She held her breath, mouth wide open, face solid red. And I thought for a moment, *She's not going to die from bleeding to death; she's going to die of suffocation because she's not breathing.* But the next moment there came from her mouth the most unbelievable high-pitched scream I had ever heard, smack into my ear.

I just held her close with all her screaming and bleeding and said quietly, "Jessica, it's going to be okay. You're going to be okay." Amazingly, she began to calm down. She gasped and shuddered but began to settle down because she knew her dad was there with his arms around her telling her everything would be fine, and she already knew she could trust him.

That's what Jesus was doing for His disciples. He was telling them as they faced the worst, "You can trust Me. I'm going to take care of you." That's what He still does today. When we are going through our worst moments, broken and screaming, He speaks peace into our situations and our hearts, and we can believe Him because He has already proven Himself credible. He tells us, "The words that you've heard Me say are true. Hold on to them. The promises that I have given, they're real. When you feel like there's nothing left, I'm there."

CONSIDERATENESS OF THE PEACE OFFERER

In these times of mega-turmoil, Jesus never dismisses our needs, never laughs at them. He considers our needs, both short-term and long-term, and He knows that our greatest need is to be with Him both now and in the future. He told us that in His Father's house are many mansions, and if that was not so, rest assured He would have told us. Then He said clearly that He was leaving in order to go there and get a place ready for us.

When we read the word *mansions* in John 14:2, we are apt to think that Jesus is picking up a hammer and nails and wood and He's building us huge houses spread all over heaven. But the actual word *mansion* is simply *dwelling place* in the original language. That is, a room. The emphasis is not on the grandness of the place but on the fact that this is home.

In Israel today we can see excavations from earlier centuries and see that they built continuous homes. When a son in a household got married, he and his bride came to live with the mom and dad, just adding on a few rooms to the parents' home. They kept adding rooms for as many people as needed a home. Everyone would be under the authority of the father because it was his house. Jesus was telling us by using this language that He is preparing a place for us just as a bridegroom would prepare a place for his bride, but that it is all a part of His Father's house. With our focus on that blessed heavenly home, in close dwelling with the Father and with Jesus, our present troubles fall into perspective. Jesus was considerate in reassuring them and us of this truth.

He didn't leave them in the dark about how they would get there. He said that if He went to prepare a place, which He's doing right now, He would come again and receive us, so that we could be where He is. He understood that when He left, they would be thrown into confusion, but the turmoil they faced or that we face today will not last forever. The turmoil that His crucifixion stirred in them was resolved when they witnessed His resurrection. Any turmoil that any of us face is eased when He speaks peace to us. The ultimate turmoil of this world will be resolved for us when He comes again.

Essentially He said, "Listen, don't worry. I'm coming back for you." What an amazing thought that is. Look at any of the major religions of the world and you see that none of the leaders even claimed to be coming back. Jesus said He is coming back, and those are words we can count on.

Look at the specific promise in 1 Thessalonians 4:13–17:

> But I do not want you to be ignorant, brethren, concerning those who have fallen asleep, lest you sorrow as others who have no hope. For if we believe that Jesus died and rose again, even so God will bring with Him those who sleep in Jesus. For this we say to you by the word of the Lord, that we who are alive and remain until the coming of the Lord will by no means precede those who are asleep. For the Lord Himself will descend from heaven with a shout, with the voice of an archangel, and with the trumpet of God. And the dead in Christ will rise first. Then we who are alive and remain shall be caught up together with them in the clouds to meet the Lord in the air. And thus we shall always be with the Lord.

Yes, one day the clouds will roll back, the trumpet will sound, and He will gather up those who belong to Him, both those who have died and those still alive. He is going to return and get us so we can spend eternity with Him.

WHAT DO WE DO WITH TURMOIL?

Let's try to grasp this peace idea as a whole. Regardless of the suffering we may be going through, we can count on Jesus. He will take care of us through the trial, and He'll someday come and take us home. We can believe this because He said it and He has proved Himself to be credible. Because He is considerate, He told us clearly about His present promise to be with us, and His future promise that we can be with Him. Because He is compassionate, He died on the cross to make our forever relationship with Him possible.

Your problem may be that your heart feels like raw hamburger; your circumstances feel like a storm at Cape Canaveral, and you don't see any way out. Sometimes it feels that it might be easier to just give in. Why trust Him when He lets us go through this stuff? Why not just deny Him, betray Him, or just give up?

Well, for one thing—let's be practical—it wouldn't do any good. You would still have a lot of hard stuff to go through, without the resources God provides. But way beyond that negative fact is the positive truth that you can take your turmoil to the One who spoke peace into the worst situation of turmoil you could imagine. You can rest in His peace and continue resting. Take another look at the wonderful promise of John 14:27: "Peace I leave with you." He is not talking about the initial peace of salvation and having your sins forgiven. It is the glorious peace that fills the heart of the person who is fully yielded to Jesus, the inner peace owned by the person who is living within the will of God. This is the peace that calms your fears and eases the extreme turmoil. This is the peace that passes understanding.

According to the University of Oslo and Norwegian Academy of Sciences, there have been more than fourteen thousand wars in the world since 3600 BC. Nations have known peace for less than 5 percent of the last 5,600 years. The U.S. Department of Defense identified forty-three combat zones in the world in 2011, up from twenty-three in 2007.[1] Peace among nations is rare.

Personal peace is perhaps even rarer. Millie Stamm of Stonecroft Ministries told of her own personal peace when she approached the writing of a book, hoping for quiet, peaceful surroundings and circumstances.

Instead, she said, God put her through one of the most difficult times of her life. She underwent two serious surgeries, and her sister became critically ill and died just before the book was finished. She also lost her husband, who died suddenly. Millie Stamm, though reeling, said, "Through these experiences I came to know God in a deeper, more personal way than I had before."[2] Although she wrote out of sorrow and ministered through pain, she experienced the peace that passes understanding as she claimed Psalm 46:10, "Be still, and know that I am God."

It's true for you and me also. His peace is our promise for today.

Questions for Individual Reflection or Small Group Discussion

1. When people are in times of stress and chaos, what are some typical reactions and responses?

2. Think back over your own life. What has been one of the greatest times of pressure for you? What happened, how did you respond, and what was the result?

3. Why do you think Jesus took His disciples away to the Upper Room at the time He did? What did He hope to accomplish during this time?

4. Talk about the significance of having Judas Iscariot, the betrayer, in the Upper Room. Why was it important that he be there? What might we learn from that experience?

5. Describe the true peace that Jesus offers. How have you experienced this in your own life?

13

WHEN JESUS PRAYS FOR YOU

John Knox was one of the great men of the Reformation movement and founder of the Presbyterian Church of Scotland. He barely avoided being burned at the stake, was imprisoned as a French galley slave, and experienced exile several times. In the late 1500s, when John Knox was on his deathbed, his wife asked him where in the Bible he would like her to read. He is said to have replied words to this effect: "Read where I first put my anchor down, in the seventeenth chapter of John."

John Knox knew from deep experience that the truths of this Bible passage can keep a person going when he faces the most trying circumstances. You and I will probably not go through the extreme trials faced by John Knox, but we continually meet situations where we don't know what to do. We have choices to make. We can go this way or that way. We can follow after God's promises and principles, or run the other way and do what the world says. In those difficult times, in the rugged mountains and deepest valleys of life, we can cling to the amazing truth that Jesus is praying for us.

As the time for His death drew near, Jesus spent some intensely personal time with His close friends in the Upper Room, underscoring for them what would be important in the days ahead. He demonstrated what it means to serve, literally getting down on His hands and knees to wash their feet. He shared the sadness of His heart, predicting that one would betray Him and one would deny Him and all would forsake Him in His hour of greatest need. Fear must have been rising in their hearts, and as they left the Upper Room together and walked into the Garden of Gethsemane, Jesus touched their point of need and promised them the great gift of peace.

He had a few more things to tell them, knowing the time was short. By then, they must have been hanging on His every word. Let's look at this time in Jesus' ministry more closely.

FAMOUS LAST WORDS

Todd Beamer, a passenger on United Flight 93 on September 11, 2001, courageously led a group of fellow passengers to storm the cockpit and thwart the highjackers' plan, causing the plane to crash into a Pennsylvania field rather than its strategic intended goal. All aboard were killed. While Todd was talking to a customer service representative on the phone from the back of the seat in front of him, his last words were: "Are you guys ready? Let's roll."[1] They are remarkable words of challenge. We might not be facing any terrorists soon, but are we ready for the role God has for us to play, whatever role in life that is? Let's embrace it with gusto. Are we ready to sacrifice whatever it takes, even our lives? Let's face our final moments with courage. Are we ready for eternity? Let's roll.

We tend to hold on to people's last words, and often they are significant. Jesus gave His friends an important single word, one of His last, in John 15, leading up to His great prayer in John 17. It's the word *remain*, found in John 15:4 and used several times in the chapter. Some translations use the word *abide*. The Greek word is *meno*, which means "to endure, to tarry, to continue, not to faint." The word is much more than a simple statement that we should stay in one place. It means stand your ground, tough it out, hang in there. It means that no matter how difficult the road is ahead, no matter what you come up against, regardless of how hard things get, you will stand.

My dad, Jerry Falwell Sr., often said, "Never, never, never quit." That is the idea Jesus was giving us in this passage. No matter what you go through, you do not quit. You stand firm. You endure to the end.

Jesus gave us this truth through an illustration taken from farm life. He called Himself the true vine; His followers, the branches; and His Father, the farmer. He told His friends that evening, and He tells us today, that branches need to stay connected to the vine if they want to produce fruit. In a vineyard, a great deal of pruning takes place and branches that don't bear fruit get snipped off so more fruit can appear. As an illustration, Jesus was not using the act of pruning to talk about losing your salvation. He was talking about fruit-bearing. Fruit is mentioned six times in the first ten verses. The bottom-line idea is that if we remain in Christ (stay connected), we will produce fruit. That fruit is listed specifically in Galatians 5:22–23, as the qualities of love, joy, peace, patience, kindness, goodness, faithfulness, gentleness, and self-control. This fruit-bearing proves that we are His children, His living branches connected to Him, enduring, and remaining in Him.

REMAINING TO THE END

Jesus went on to tell His friends the reason behind giving them the concept embodied in the word *remain*. It's all about joy. He told them He had shared these truths so that they would be filled with His joy. In summary, Jesus said, "I want you to understand how important it is that you stick with Me no matter how difficult the road ahead might be. Stay with Me and you will produce fruit and you will spill over with My joy." He knew things were going to get incredibly tough for them in the next few hours and days, and He knows things often get tough for us. His word to us is, stay committed. Don't quit. It's likely that Jesus and His disciples walked through vineyards as they went into the olive grove of the Garden of Gethsemane, so right there at hand was a living illustration of His words. He may have pointed to luscious grapes hanging down from a branch that was well connected to the vine, or a withered branch that had been cast aside and had no fruit. The words came alive for them.

A few years ago my wife, Shari, and the kids went to visit her family, and I stayed home by myself for a few weeks. As we said good-bye, she reminded me to make sure to water the house plants.

On my first day alone I picked up some take-out food for dinner, sat down at the table, ate, and left all the trash on the table. I thought, *It's just me. The mess doesn't matter.* Day after day I did this until food containers were piled all over.

The day before Shari was due home, I left work early, rushed home, and cleaned the house. I wanted to impress her that I had everything under control. But as I cleaned up the kitchen, guess what my eyes fell on? Several house plants that were not happy. I ran for water and poured it into those languishing plants, hoping they would revive and Shari would never know that I had forgotten all about them. But it didn't do one bit of good. When Shari walked in, the first things she noticed were her dead plants.

It's a picture of the way many of us think we can live the Christian life. We think our messes don't matter. We go merrily along when life is smooth, and we neglect the things that make for growth and health and fruit. When problems start to rear their heads, we panic. We run for the water, thinking we can find some kind of quick fix for our languishing spiritual lives. Jesus told us here that's not the way to live. Instead, we need to remain in Him every day, stay connected in good days and bad, keep plugged into Him, keep the water and nutrition flowing, and experience His joy.

Jesus added that if His followers chose not to stay connected to Him, they would not be able to do anything at all. John 15:5 says, "Without Me you can do nothing." But wait a minute—there are people who don't even know Christ, and we can't say they are doing nothing. They work at jobs, they make money, some are highly successful, they have relationships, and some are good at relationships. Some are even good at charity. What does He mean that apart from Him we can do nothing? Jesus was not talking about what you and I can accomplish on a daily basis, what tasks we can perform, what skills we can exercise, or how fast we can tick off our to-do lists. He was saying that we will accomplish nothing of eternal value unless what we do is based on the resources God gives. Without the life of Jesus flowing through us, our accomplishments don't amount to a hill of beans.

Just a few days before I wrote these words, I was standing in the hospital room of my uncle, Sam Pate. He had been growing sicker and sicker, and the doctor had finally told the family that my uncle had only days left, maybe hours, before he would slip into heaven. On Thursday and Friday of his last week, Sam talked with all of us and actually laughed with us. We had a wonderful time together as family. But his illness progressed to the point where he could not speak. His eyes closed, and we could see that he was slowly slipping away as we watched.

About that time the door of the hospital room opened, and the nurse came in. Suddenly my uncle opened his eyes. He said in his normal strong voice to the nurse, "Do you know that God loves you?" We were all shocked at his sudden energy. The nurse replied, "Well, yes, Mr. Pate, I do know that God loves me." Then he said, "Good, because God loves you." Someone in the room turned the question to my uncle and asked him, "Well, do *you* love God?" And he said with perfect clarity, "Absolutely, oh, I love God." Then he added, "And I can see God." He closed his eyes, and not long after that he slipped into heaven.

I can't think of a more perfect way to face death than the way Sam faced it. Like him, I want to stick with God even to my last breath. I want to remain in Him.

JESUS PRAYED FOR HIMSELF

Jesus closed this introduction to His final message with a warning that the world will hate the disciples just as it hated and rejected Him. He promised the Holy Spirit would come and ministr to them in amazing ways, and then He assured His friends that their grief about His leaving would ultimately turn to joy. That's all recorded in John 15–16. Then He entered the sanctuary.

The sanctuary for Jesus was anywhere that He happened to be when He turned His heart to the Father in prayer. That is where it is for us too. On this occasion the sanctuary for Jesus was an olive grove. John 17:1 says, "Jesus spoke these words, lifted up His eyes to heaven, and said . . ."

In those days the posture of prayer was a little different from ours. When we pray, we usually bow our heads and close our eyes. Sometimes we get on our knees before God. Sometimes we lie face-down before God. But the customary way of praying in those days was to lift up the head toward heaven and look up with open eyes. When Jesus stood at the grave of Lazarus, recorded in John 11, Jesus lifted up His eyes and spoke to the Father. That's what He did here in Gethsemane in the disciples' hearing, as He began this prayer, the longest prayer recorded in the Bible. This is the true Lord's Prayer, for it is the definitive prayer that He Himself spoke. The one we usually call the Lord's Prayer that begins, "Our Father in heaven . . . ," recorded in Matthew 6:9–13, is really a pattern prayer that Jesus gave His followers to speak.

The first thing Jesus did in Gethsemane was to pray for Himself: "Father, the hour has come. Glorify Your Son, that Your Son also may glorify You" (John 17:1). He knew that He had shared all the truths with the disciples He needed to, that the work the Father had given Him was nearly completed, and that the time was now upon Him when He could return to the Father.

The specific work that Jesus had accomplished so far was offered to the Father: "As You have given Him authority over all flesh, that He should give eternal life to as many as You have given Him. And this is eternal life, that they may know You, the only true God, and Jesus Christ whom You have sent. I have glorified You on the earth. I have finished the work which You have given Me to do" (John 17:2–4). In other words, Jesus had brought people to eternal life, to salvation, and this accomplishment was presented to the Father.

"And now, O Father, glorify Me together with Yourself, with the glory which I had with You before the world was" (John 17:5). While Jesus was on this earth living among us as one of us, He had to veil His glory. Philippians 2 explains more fully the *kenosis*, a Greek word meaning the "emptying" out of Jesus when He came to earth. Now it was time for His glory to be restored.

Notice that it is not out of line nor a mark of selfishness to pray for yourself. In fact, it is always true that, as an old spiritual puts it,

"It's me, it's me, it's me, O Lord, standing in the need of prayer." Before we can rightly pray for others, we need to pray for ourselves and get our hearts in tune with heaven. Jesus was asking here that the Father would bring Him into the glorious state that they had shared before the world began.

JESUS PRAYED FOR HIS DISCIPLES

Jesus didn't stop after He had prayed for Himself, as we sometimes do. He prayed for His disciples, the friends who walked that road into Gethsemane with Him.

I pray for them. I do not pray for the world but for those whom You have given Me, for they are Yours. And all Mine are Yours, and Yours are Mine, and I am glorified in them. Now I am no longer in the world, but these are in the world, and I come to You. Holy Father, keep through Your name those whom You have given Me, that they may be one as We are. While I was with them in the world, I kept them in Your name. Those whom You gave Me I have kept; and none of them is lost except the son of perdition [Judas Iscariot], that the Scripture might be fulfilled. (John 17:9–12)

Jesus prayed four specific requests for His friends that day.

1. **He prayed for protection.** How encouraging it is to you and me to realize that Jesus prayed for His disciples' protection, as they faced the days ahead. He prayed the Father would just wrap them up with His love and care.
2. **He prayed for unity.** He prayed that they would be one, that they would experience the kind of oneness that the Father and Son experienced. This is not an organizational unity; it's an organic unity, which nothing can really destroy. It exists even when believers have squabbles among themselves.
3. **He prayed for keeping.** Jesus asked the Father that His friends would be kept, held on to, not lost. His children certainly will

be kept because they are sealed with the Holy Spirit and because
the Savior is constantly praying for them. In John 10:28, Jesus
said, "No one can snatch them out of my hand," and in verses
29–30 He added, "No one can snatch them out of my Father's
hand. I and the Father are one" (NIV).

4. **He prayed for joy.** In the next part of the passage, Jesus
   clearly asks the Father that His own joy may be fulfilled in His
   friends. This will come about as they internalize His Word.
   They will be in the world but not of it, and kept from the evil
   one. They'll be sanctified by the truth of God's Word. All this
   will enable them to be sent by Jesus into the world, just as the
   Father sent Him.

JESUS PRAYED FOR YOU AND ME

As He walked toward the Garden of Gethsemane that night, Jesus
looked ahead in time and prayed for you and me. In case we may
think that this prayer of Jesus was only for followers of that day, He
said very specifically, "I do not pray for these alone, but also for those
who will believe in Me through their word; that they all may be one,
as You, Father, are in Me, and I in You; that they also may be one in
Us, that the world may believe that You sent Me" (John 17:20–21).

Jesus assured us in this passage that He was praying not just for
those walking the road with Him that night but also for those who
would hear the message of the gospel from those early disciples after
they were energized by the resurrection and indwelt by the Holy Spirit.
He was also praying for those who would take the message farther,
who would share it with friends and children and grandchildren, who
would take it to different places and other cultures and pass it down
the generations. He was praying for all who would eventually believe
down through history as the gospel went from continent to continent
around the world. He was praying for you, that when you heard the
gospel, you would believe.

It is amazing to think that as Jesus took these last steps, traveling that road from the Upper Room, walking to the garden where

He would be arrested and led away to His death, Jesus was thinking about you and me. He knew what we would someday be called to go through; He knew the hatred and misunderstanding we would face; He knew the struggles and the challenges that we would meet in our individual lives. He knew about our broken hearts, our prisons, our poverty, and our blindness. Knowing it all, Jesus asked the Father to protect us and to be with us.

And He goes on praying for us today. The writer to the Hebrews tells us, "He always lives to make intercession for them" (Heb. 7:25).

LIVING OUT THE JESUS PRAYER

Let's recap: In His last intimate conversation with His followers, Jesus reminded them and reminds us to remain connected to Him. If we want power, we have to be plugged in and stay there. He told us to stick with Him no matter what, and we will have not only power but joy.

As we listen closely to His prayer, we see His desires for us: He wants us to live in unity, the unity that is the organic result of us all being connected to Him. He wants us to be protected and kept, and that is His business. He will do it. As we look at the pattern of His prayer, we see how He wants us to pray for one another, as our lives grow into conformity to His image. Are Jesus' prayers answered? Every single one.

Questions for Individual Reflection or Small Group Discussion

1. What passage of Scripture would you most like to have read to you just before you die, and why?
2. Describe what it means to "abide" in Christ.
3. The promise in Scripture is that if we abide in Christ, we will bear fruit. What does this "fruit" look like?
4. In what specific ways do you need to never give up?
5. "We will accomplish nothing of eternal value unless what we do is based on the resources God gives." Discuss this important idea and how it relates to your life.

14

SEVEN MESSAGES FROM THE CROSS

About three hundred years ago Franz Joseph Haydn was commissioned to write music to describe the seven last sayings of Jesus Christ from the cross, music that would inspire understanding and devotion. He produced an oratorio called *The Seven Last Words of Christ* that continues to transform people from a broad spectrum of faith experience. The music is performed by full orchestras and choirs around the world. The setting for the original composition was Spain, a country that had recently experienced disastrous earthquakes. So Haydn finished his oratorio with music that fittingly depicted the biblical earthquake that marked the death of Jesus.

In 1994, the Vermeer String Quartet performed Haydn's *Seven Last Words of Christ* with devotional meditations interspersed with the music, recorded in the book *Echoes from Calvary* by Richard Young. One meditation was provided by a woman named Kelly Clem just after Palm Sunday 1994, the day a tornado had hit her rural Alabama church. It spared her and 123 other worshipers, including her youngest child. But the storm took the lives of nineteen others, including Kelly Clem's older daughter. The *New York Times* reported that Clem began her meditation with the words, "It is perhaps the most difficult thing a mother should ever have to face: watching her own child's death."[1] Her meditation prefaced the Haydn music on the words of Jesus to His own mother, as Mary stood at the foot of the cross watching Him die. Perhaps no one can more deeply understand Mary's feelings at that time than a mother who has lost her child.

We are going to look at Jesus' final words to Mary and the other last words He spoke as He hung suspended between earth and heaven, dying. This would be Jesus' crowning achievement, the purpose for His coming. Dying was the mission for which He came to earth, for which He marched up Calvary that day. As we have been looking at the 1,000-day ministry of Jesus, it all points to this event. We want to look very deeply at His dying words. If we have heard them before, we want to learn them again at a deeper level that engages our whole being. If we have never heard them before, we want to learn them in their fresh passion and let them impact us profoundly.

His dying words are so important for us; they are words we can cling to for all eternity.

THE ROAD TO THE CROSS

Leading up to the cross in the last few chapters, we have traveled with the crowds with Jesus and His friends into Jerusalem in what He knew was a superficial kind of triumph, we went with Him into the Upper Room with the Twelve for a personal time, and we walked with them into the Garden of Gethsemane. Jesus in foreknowledge understood the pain He was about to experience. He asked His Father to let the cup of agony pass from Him but submitted Himself, nevertheless, to God's will.

Then Judas arrived. Remember Judas had slipped out of the Upper Room. At this point he came back, bringing the Roman soldiers. He kissed Jesus on the cheek to identify the one they wanted. The soldiers grabbed Jesus, tied Him up, captured Him there in the garden, and led Him to face Caiaphas, the high priest. Jesus went through a trial, was mocked, and then was beaten. He was dragged off for another trial before Pilate, the Roman governor. Pilate couldn't figure out why Jesus had been brought before him. Even Pilate's own wife warned him to have nothing to do with Jesus because she'd had bad dreams about Him. Pilate even washed his hands of the whole matter, as if a little soap and water would secure his innocence.

Pilate presented Jesus to the people, thinking they would agree to Jesus' release as the token prisoner customarily freed to mark Passover. But instead the crowd called for the release of Barabbas, a murderer who was condemned to die. Pilate asked the crowd what he should do with Jesus, and the crowd yelled, "Crucify Him! Crucify Him!" This crowd no doubt contained some of the same ones who cried out just a few days before, "Hosanna!" Pilate gave in to the crowd's wishes, and Jesus was hauled off to the Praetorium in the Antonia Fortress and beaten again. There in the courtyard the Roman soldiers crowned Him with thorns, put a purple robe around Him, mocked Him, took a reed and slapped Him in the face with it, spit on Him, and then placed a cross on His back and ordered Him to carry it up the road toward Golgotha, which in Hebrew means the Place of the Skull.

At Golgotha, called Calvary in the Greek language, they laid Him down on the cross and took big spikes and pounded them through the bones in His hands and feet, nailing Him to that cross. They lifted the cross up and plunked it into a hole they had dug. They put a banner across the top that said "This Is Jesus the King of the Jews" (Matt. 27:37), and they left Him to die.

Roman soldiers continued the abuse, taunting Him to come down from the cross, if He really was so great, or call angels to rescue Him or Elijah to help Him. They made a game of gambling for His clothing, not knowing they were fulfilling prophecy. As the soldiers mocked, the religious leaders must have beamed, thinking they had won. The disciples and other friends cowered in fear. They were bewildered about why Jesus was hanging there dying, the One they had believed was God the Son.

Mary, His own mother, was with some of the other Christ-followers, and she must have looked up at the cross with a broken heart and tears streaming down her face. She may have remembered the angel's announcement of His supernatural birth, her joy when she laid Him in the manger, the bright star that marked the place where He lay. She may have remembered holding her tiny king as He slept, teaching Him to walk, watching Him grow up, wise beyond His years. She may have recalled how her heart wrenched when He said He must go about His Father's business, but she let Him go and His teaching spread. Some of His miracles she had seen with her own eyes; many more she had heard about. Then she had heard the terrible news that Jesus was on trial. By the time she arrived, He was broken and bleeding, His body lifted on a cross that had been jolted into place.

As Mary stood there weeping, she and the others heard Jesus' final words before He died. We often gather in hospital rooms or at bedsides, places where loved ones are about to slip into the presence of God. We sit at their sides, clinging to every word because we want to hear important words. We hope we can catch what they are saying in those last moments of life. Those words are so meaningful because those are the dying words. They are the last we will ever hear from them in this life.

People don't always manage to speak profound words as their last, but Jesus' dying words were highly important. They wrapped up all the words He had spoken in parables and sermons as He had journeyed through the 1,000-day ministry. These seven statements spoken by Jesus as He hung there on the cross offer one of the most vivid displays ever of God's power. These statements form a summary of the way Jesus invites us to live.

STATEMENT #1: A DISPLAY OF SUPERNATURAL FORGIVENESS

The first words Jesus spoke on that black day were: "Father, forgive them, for they do not know what they do" (Luke 23:34).

The statement as recorded was prefaced by the simple words, "Jesus said." *Said*, in the original language, is not just a past tense, referring to words that He spoke and that's all there was to it. It means an imperfective kind of action. We could translate it this way: "Jesus was continually saying, 'Father, forgive them. Father, forgive them. Father, forgive them."

Those first words Jesus spoke on the cross are words that He continues to say today as He intercedes for you and me. The fact that His arms were stretched wide on the cross is more than just part of the execution method. It's a symbol of Jesus' all-embracing forgiveness continually extended to all who will receive it, both then and now.

Maybe you are aware that you, like me, have done a lot of stupid things. You have made dumb decisions, regretted foolish mistakes, and—yes, let's call it what it is—committed sins. We are not proud of them; sometimes we are embarrassed, and when we begin to realize how serious they actually are, we may feel acute remorse. For all these Jesus extended forgiveness.

This cry of Jesus shows His divine mercy, something every one of us needs desperately. It also models for us how we need to be merciful and extend forgiveness to others as we allow Him to live His life through us.

Louis Zamperini's incredible story of survival and determination is told in the book *Unbroken* by Laura Hillenbrand. As a prisoner of war in Japan during World War II, Louis suffered unspeakably, especially at the hands of one official whom prisoners nicknamed the Bird. It would be hard to imagine a hell bad enough for a man who inflicted such torment on his fellow men. But Louis survived, and after the war came home to America and regained his health. Nonetheless, he took to alcohol and developed a murderous hatred for the Bird. The man, whose real name was Mutsuhiro Watanabe, continually escaped the justice of a war crimes tribunal and was still at large. Louis made it his life mission to find and murder the Bird, and the hatred nearly destroyed him.

Then in 1949, Louis became a Christian at a Billy Graham crusade. He immediately lost his taste for alcohol and more deeply, lost his taste for murder. He had a new life mission—to find and extend forgiveness to the Bird. In the early 1950s, he traveled to Japan and shared the gospel with many former prison guards, often throwing his arms around them. But many years went by, and Louis never was able to find the Bird. As an old man Louis went back to Japan to light the torch in the 1998 Olympics, reminiscent of his own Olympic career that had been cut short by war. While there he learned that the Bird had also lived out his life a free man, and Louis learned his whereabouts. Louis carried a letter that carefully explained the gospel of forgiveness, told his former captor about Jesus' love, and said that Louis also wanted to extend forgiveness to him. The Bird refused to meet Louis but did accept the letter. It is not known whether the Bird ever accepted the forgiveness of Louis or of Jesus. But the story underlines how massive is the forgiveness Jesus offers, even channeled through one of His children.[2]

STATEMENT #2: A DISPLAY OF SUPERNATURAL COMPASSION

The second sentence Jesus shared from the cross was: "Today you will be with Me in Paradise" (Luke 23:43). Jesus spoke these words to a man hanging next to Him, also being crucified. He assured the man that before the day was out, they would both be in paradise.

We know from the record that two other men were crucified along with Jesus. Both were criminals, and both mocked Jesus at the start. One continued to spew blasphemy, demanding with taunts that if Jesus really was the Son of God, He would save Himself and them. But the other man warned him to respect God, and noted the two of them were suffering the just rewards of their deeds. Then he revealed the beginnings of faith by saying, "This Man has done nothing wrong" (Luke 23:41). He could see that Jesus didn't have any sin of His own to die for, which qualified Him to die for the sins of others. The man didn't stop there, but turned his words to Jesus and asked, "Lord, remember me when You come into Your kingdom" (Luke 23:42). He was begging for help and for hope. Many scholars believe that this man was a murderer and possibly a partner in crime with Barabbas. The man may have recognized that Jesus was dying in place of Barabbas. Maybe that sparked the realization that Jesus was also dying in his place in the ultimate sense, dying for his eternal forgiveness.

Possibly we think that murder is the worst thing a person can possibly commit. But even for a murderer, Jesus said, "I can forgive even that." Whatever it is that we have done, whatever evil rumbles in our hearts threatening to express itself, Jesus offers forgiveness.

The story of the man dying beside Jesus, thief or murderer or both, forever debunks the idea that we need to pile up a lot of good works to earn salvation. He simply was out of time. His faith alone, a faith that was new and tiny, secured for him a place with Jesus in paradise. Jesus' promise to this man was beyond natural. The natural thing is to see that people get their just desserts and be glad about it. Supernatural divine compassion is revealed in Jesus' words to him. It is a compassion we can also count on when we need it most.

STATEMENT #3: A DISPLAY OF SUPERNATURAL CARING

The third dying statement of Jesus was partly spoken to His mother, indicating that she should now look to John as a son, and partly spoken to John, indicating that he should adopt Mary as his own mother.

"When Jesus therefore saw His mother, and the disciple whom He loved standing by, He said to His mother, 'Woman, behold your son!' Then He said to the disciple, 'Behold your mother!'" (John 19:26–27). This moment holds an incredible display of supernatural love. Jesus, even in dying, ensured that everything would be taken care of; He met the needs of those who depended on Him. Instead of focusing on His own pain, He gave caring attention to those who would be left behind.

It reminds us a little of what took place on September 11, 2001. We have all seen the images and heard the stories of firefighters who rushed into the World Trade Center as everyone else was trying to rush out. They entered those buildings without any consideration for their own safety. They were simply bent on doing everything possible to rescue those who were in the middle of that inferno. They did not focus on their own welfare.

When Jesus hung on that cross dying, He did a similar act but took it to the ultimate degree. He took care of others. In that moment

He displayed love that goes way beyond the natural level. The scene was like that of a father calling his family together moments before his death and saying to the eldest son, "Listen, you're the man of the house now; you take care of the family. You handle all the situations that arise. You manage the business." In his supernatural caring Jesus made it clear that although He would soon be gone from their presence, they would be cared for. And that includes you and me.

Statement #4: A Display of Supernatural Commitment

The fourth statement Jesus made that day was, "My God, My God, why have You forsaken Me?" He cried out in the midst of His worst pain and suffering, at about the ninth hour of the day, noon by the reckoning of those times. Matthew 27:46 says, "And about the ninth hour Jesus cried out with a loud voice, saying, 'Eli, Eli, lama sabachthani?' that is, 'My God, My God, why have You forsaken Me?'"

It was a rhetorical question; that is, Jesus knew the answer. Separation in the Godhead had to take place because that is infinite spiritual death; that is the kind of death that substitutes for us and saves us. Jesus spoke these words from the worst of His agony. The beating, mocking, crown of thorns, nails hammered through His flesh—it was unspeakably horrible. But there was something worse to come. Jesus could have struck all His enemies dead in a second, stopping this torment. But He had committed Himself to the plan since before the earth's creation; He had committed Himself to His Father's will in the Garden of Gethsemane; and on the cross He committed Himself again to completing the job He had been sent to do. He would go through the infinite death. Far worse than physical suffering was the spiritual pain. In that bleak moment, all the punishment for all the sins of all the world was laid on Him, and hell threw everything it had at Him. Jesus could have said, "Stop!" But He didn't.

Instead, He had stopped those who wanted to fight this chain of events. In the garden when soldiers came to arrest Jesus, the disciples drew swords. One cut off the ear of a man named Malchus. Jesus called that to a stop, restored the man's ear, and continued resolutely toward Calvary. He was committed.

STATEMENT #5: A DISPLAY OF REAL HUMANITY

The next words Jesus spoke from the cross form a simple statement that reveals His humanity. He said, "I thirst." The full statement from John 19:28 reads, "After this, Jesus, knowing that all things were now accomplished, that the Scripture might be fulfilled, said, 'I thirst!'"

This is God the Son, who created with His Father all the rivers, oceans, and groundwater, and who planned and set in motion the pattern of rainfall. Yet He was thirsty. It shows that He was 100 percent human, just as at the same time He was 100 percent God. In His humanness, Jesus experienced all the sensations that we experience. He was thirsty.

He was mindful that scriptures were being fulfilled. The Old Testament predicts Messiah's crucifixion over and over. Bible scholar Dr. J. Vernon McGee said that twenty-eight prophecies were fulfilled while Jesus hung on the cross. His thirst fulfilled the prophecy of Psalm 69:21.

We can be greatly glad that Jesus displayed His humanity on the cross. He proved to us that the God of the universe became fully human. He walked out of heaven's splendor and became one of us. Jesus needed to be fully human so He could be a perfect substitute for humans. He also needed to be fully God, for God is infinite, and in that infiniteness Jesus could substitute not just for one human but for all humans for all time.

STATEMENT #6: A DISPLAY OF SUPERNATURAL VICTORY

In John 19:30, "[Jesus] said, 'It is finished!' And bowing His head, He gave up His spirit." The word *finished* in the original language is *tetelestai*, which means "a past completed action that has continual and enduring results." This is the same word that would have been used in that day by an artist or sculptor when he had created an incredible piece of art. Hours and hours would go into making it absolutely perfect, and when the artist felt he was done, he would step back and look at the piece and say, "Yes, that's it. It is finished. It's perfect."

We sometimes use similar language when we are deeply satisfied with something. We may say, "It's a keeper." Recently Shari and I were cleaning out the garage and came across a box that had been stuck in a corner for years. We dug through it and sorted things to toss, things for a garage sale, and things to keep. In the bottom of the box was a notebook with a picture drawn by our daughter, Jessica, when she was about three or four years old. She had drawn one big body and little sticks for arms and legs. I remembered the day she had drawn it, working so hard. The face turned out massive and misshapen. Then she colored the picture—the skin a perfect shade of orange. When she felt satisfied, she held it up and said, "Dad, what do you think?" And of course I said, "Oh, it is beautiful. It is perfect." To Shari that day in the garage, I said, "We're keeping this."

That is a small picture of what Jesus meant when He said, "Tetelestai." It is as if He took a step back from His work at the cross that He had just painted with such agony in His own blood, and He saw that it was perfect. It had accomplished all it needed to do and was a completed action with continual, enduring results. It was a keeper. Jesus chose His simple words carefully so that we would know the action that took place that day was action that still works today.

STATEMENT #7: A DISPLAY OF SUPERNATURAL SECURITY

The final words Jesus spoke on the cross that day just before He died are found in Luke 23:46: "When Jesus had cried out with a loud voice, He said, 'Father, "into your hands I commit My spirit."' Having said this, He breathed His last."

The gospel writer Luke was a doctor. He had no doubt been at the bedside of many people in their final moments, and he knew how people died: often with a death rattle, often with a struggle against the inevitable, and if they speak it is usually with a faint voice. But Jesus cried out in a loud voice His statement of victory that His work was done, not in a raspy, thin voice like a man whose life was ebbing away. Jesus did not struggle against death but went to the cross willingly. In His last moment on the cross, He dismissed His spirit. He chose the moment of His death. It's as if He said to Himself, "Away You go."

Jesus used the last breath in His human body to place His spirit in the hands of His Father. By this, Jesus displayed to all who gathered there and to us today, that supernatural security is found in the hands of almighty God. That is the only place to be. When we come to that last moment of life, when we take that last breath and slip into eternity, we can trust God fully. Jesus' dying words made that so clear. His battle was won, His work was finished, and it will be finished forever. We can trust ourselves into the Father's hands.

Jesus speaks this same kind of assurance into our lives today if we will hear Him. He speaks forgiveness, compassion, caring, and commitment. He touches our humanity and pronounces victory over sin and forever security.

A story is told of a young woman, Jane, who knocked on the door of her neighbor, Sue. Jane needed to tell Sue that a little boy in the classroom that both their sons attended had suddenly died that day. Sue's child had been absent with a little cold, and Jane didn't want him to go to school the next day with no preparation. Both women felt deeply for and identified with the bereaved parents because they, too, had sons the same age. Sue, not a believer, expressed shock and horror. Jane told her that the child who died and his parents were Christians.

As the two women shared coffee, Jane explained that the child's parents had expressed peace because of their faith in Christ and confidence in a home in heaven. Sue shook her head thoughtfully and said, "That's where you Christians have it all over everyone else—when it comes to dying."

She got that absolutely right. Let's give Jesus our grateful hearts.

QUESTIONS FOR INDIVIDUAL REFLECTION
OR SMALL GROUP DISCUSSION

1. What would you like your last words before dying to be?
2. Talk about the kind of forgiveness that Jesus both modeled for us and encouraged us to have for other people. What is this forgiveness like? How have you seen it lived out in your own life? Who is someone you perhaps need to forgive?
3. When Jesus cried out, "My God, My God, why have You forsaken Me?" what did this mean? How could God the Father have forsaken God the Son?
4. When Jesus said on the cross, "It is finished," what did this mean, both then and for us today?
5. How can we be peaceful, even in the face of death?

15

THE LOUDEST
SERMON EVER

The loudest sermon ever delivered by anyone was given without a word: Jesus simply walked out of His own grave. That act said, "Jesus wins!"

We have looked at many incidents in Jesus' life in this journey through His 1,000-day ministry, and we have discussed some implications for our lives today, but let's go away from this book with one big thought in mind: Jesus wins, and because He wins, we can win. You and I can be victorious people.

Bruce and Brian, two young boys in seventh grade, both excelled at track. The boys were twins and bonded deeply to one another, so the fact that their interest in track was mutual was no surprise. It did mean they often competed against one another. One day both were scheduled to run in the 1,500-yard race in the spring championship track meet for their district. They set off together at the starting gun and rounded the track almost neck and neck, both beaming. First Bruce pulled ahead, then Brian, but both were ahead of the pack. As they neared the finish line, Bruce led by a few feet. Then he stumbled and fell. The crowd gasped. Brian could have surged ahead and easily won the race, but he did what his instinct told him to do. He stopped and helped his brother get up, brushed him off, and ran the rest of the way with him. Another runner flashed by them and crossed the finish line in first place.

In one sense both the twins lost. Or did they both win? There are many kinds of victory, and the victory we are talking about in this chapter is the kind that Jesus taught, the kind that puts doing right ahead of being first, that puts kindness and the other fruits of the Holy Spirit far ahead of ambition and achievement.

Two Kinds of Victory

Because of Jesus' resurrection, we can be winners. He gives us victory in at least two ways:

1. We Win Peace and Purpose

We took the first step away from loser-mode when we received Jesus as Savior. As we move out and explore the Christian life, we find it's not about climbing one mountain after another to satisfy our inner restlessness. That emptiness has been filled by Jesus. Instead of working to stifle an inner hunger, we can turn our attention to climbing the mountains He lays out for us, meeting the challenges that fulfill us and that build into His plan for our lives.

2. We Win Living as Jesus Lived

We have looked closely at Jesus' 1,000-day ministry, and I hope you will continue to explore the Bible, with careful attention to His life and teachings. As we retrace His steps again and again, we find ourselves going deeper into our relationship with Him. We begin to understand at new levels what it means to be contented, how to experience calmed storms, how to overcome temptation, how to share our faith—in short, how to follow Him. It's true that living as Jesus lived is a tall order. Someone has said the Christian life is not difficult; it's impossible. However, it is Him-possible. That means we truly can live as He lived as we allow the resurrected Jesus to live His life through us.

It is all possible because of the resurrection. What if Jesus had not walked out of the tomb that day? The implications are huge. For example, we would have the model of a fine life and good teachings that Jesus left us but no power to follow them. Second, we would have a major puzzle on our hands: we would have the promises that Jesus is the Lamb of God but be without the effect of the perfect lamb's sacrifice. In the temple, officials took lambs that were brought and led them to the altar, where they were killed and laid out to burn in sacrifice to cover the people's sins. Many of those lambs had been raised in Bethlehem, just seven miles from Jerusalem. Bethlehem was the sheep industry capital of the country, and an important economic engine in Bethlehem was raising temple lambs. More than 250,000 lambs were raised in Bethlehem annually. It's interesting that God the Son chose to enter the world at Bethlehem, the lamb center. Fast-forward thirty years. Jesus approached John the Baptist to ask for His own baptism. John recognized who Jesus was and said, "Behold! The Lamb of God who takes away the sin of the world!" (John 1:29). About 1,000 days later, that perfect Lamb was sacrificed to pay forever for the sins of all mankind.

But if Jesus had stayed dead, it would have been a different story, and everything would come crumbling down around us. We would never know if the sacrifice had been accepted by God the Father. We would never know if Jesus was who He said He was. We would never know if we could be with Him in paradise as He had promised the thief who died beside Him. If Jesus did not rise from the dead, the underpinnings of civilization would crumble because most of what is noble and good in society is based on this principle. We would have to doubt all Jesus' promises. He had said that He would be abused and killed and then would rise again on the third day. Luke 18:31–33 says that He took the Twelve aside and told them, "We are going up to Jerusalem, and all things that are written by the prophets concerning the Son of Man will be accomplished. For He will be delivered to the Gentiles and will be mocked and insulted and spit upon. They will scourge Him and kill Him. And the third day He will rise again." If that had not truly happened, we'd have to conclude that Jesus was wrong about other things too.

WHAT REALLY HAPPENED?

The disciples had watched the abuse being heaped on Jesus, and they had watched Him die. But they didn't remember or understand

His prediction, so after He died they hid, fearing for their lives too. Shortly after Jesus had spoken His last words and breathed His last breath, a man named Joseph of Arimathea, helped by Nicodemus, intervened to do what he could, to see that Jesus' body got a decent burial.

Luke 23:52–53 says, "This man went to Pilate and asked for the body of Jesus. Then he took it down, wrapped it in linen, and laid it in a tomb that was hewn out of the rock, where no one had ever lain before." The women who had followed Jesus in life followed His body and saw where the tomb was located. They went home to prepare spices and oils for further anointing of the body, and they rested throughout that long Sabbath day.

On the third day the sun rose and with it the hope of all mankind. On the third day Mary Magdalene was first to arrive at the tomb and see that the stone was not in place. She ran and told Peter and John, who hurried to the tomb. The other women came bringing their spices and oils and also found the stone rolled away. When they went inside and did not find Jesus' body, they were totally perplexed. Suddenly two men (probably angels, although they looked like men), wearing shining garments, stood beside the women and said, "Why do you seek the living among the dead? He is not here, but is risen! Remember how He spoke to you when He was still in Galilee, saying, 'The Son of Man must be delivered into the hands of sinful men, and be crucified, and the third day rise again'" (Luke 24:5–7).

With that angelic review the friends of Jesus remembered His words, and those words began to make sense to them. They ran and told these things to the disciples and the other followers, and things started to click.

Of course, in order to verify a resurrection story, the person missing from the grave has to be seen by witnesses. Otherwise we just have a case of a missing body. The person who sees and reports can't be someone given to hallucinations and not someone who simply dreams about seeing the dead man walking. There are certainly eyewitnesses in the case of Jesus. Ten distinct appearances of Jesus are recorded after His resurrection. He appeared to Mary Magdalene, to some other women, to Peter, to two disciples on the road to Emmaus, to ten disciples, to a group of eleven disciples, to five hundred people at one time, to James, and to the eleven disciples two more times. The variety of people and circumstances involved in the appearances are just too great for people to be making this up, pointed out Dr. Gary Habermas, professor of theology and consultant to Thomas Road Baptist Church. Habermas has studied the evidence carefully and says there are about two dozen reasons to accept the historicity of the empty tomb.

WHAT DIDN'T HAPPEN?

There is a notion that maybe Jesus didn't actually die; rather, He just fainted, and the cool air of the tomb revived Him. But friends and enemies alike were convinced that He had died. The Romans didn't bother to break His legs, as they customarily did to crucifixion victims to hurry their deaths along, because they saw that Jesus was already dead. Nicodemus and Joseph of Arimathea were certainly convinced He was dead and had close-up opportunity to see that it was so as they carried the body to the tomb. The writers of the Gospels were all convinced Jesus had died. If He had not died on the cross, the linen wrappings and heavy ointments would have suffocated Him. And the idea that a man who had gone through the torture He had experienced might get up and roll away that stone from the inside is simply ridiculous.

Everybody agreed He had died, and everybody agreed the tomb was empty on the morning of the third day. Some have tried to explain it as a case of grave-robbing. Indeed, there were people who dug up graves to rob the bodies of any finery that might have been buried with them. But Jesus was known to be a poor man; it would hardly be worth the risk of confronting the Roman guards to check for trinkets. And why make off with the whole body?

If Jesus' body had been stolen, it would have to be either His friends or His enemies who did it. Some have said His friends did it to try to convince people that He had risen because He had predicted that He would. They could have gotten quite a cult going that way. But that idea doesn't hold water. First, the Romans had sealed the tomb and placed a guard of soldiers around it. Not just one but sixteen soldiers made up a guard contingent, so probably four at a time stood guard in shifts around the clock. They were tough, highly trained warriors, heavily armed. The scenario of a few disciples overwhelming them, breaking the seal of Rome on the stone, which in itself brought a death penalty, is foolishness. Especially for the sake of a lie. Later the disciples faced torture and some faced death rather than confess that they had staged the resurrection. Yet the guards were paid by the religious authorities to perpetuate the lie that the disciples stole Jesus' body while they slept. Oh yes, sleeping on the job was another offense punishable by death.

Others say Jesus' enemies may have stolen the body, but that also fails in logic. Both Jews and Romans wanted Him dead. A few weeks later when Peter preached the resurrection at Pentecost, the Jews and Romans could have stopped the new church in its tracks, squashed it before it ever got off the ground if they had produced the body of Jesus. They didn't do it because they didn't have it.

As for Jesus' appearances, the idea that they were hallucinations falls apart. Too many people saw Him. They touched Him and saw Him eat and heard Him speak. The people who saw Him were not expecting it; on the contrary, they were skeptical and disillusioned. Some were not even believers. For example, James, the half brother of Jesus, was at that time still a skeptic. "The variety of circumstances defy the possibility of explaining away the eyewitness accounts as psychological hallucinations," said Dr. Dan Hayden.[1]

Thomas Arnold, a professor of history at Oxford University, who wrote a three-volume history about ancient Rome, said, "I have been used for many years to study the history of other times, and to examine and weigh the evidence of those who have written about them; and I know of no fact in the history of mankind which is proved by better and fuller evidence of every sort, to the understanding of a fair inquirer, than that Christ died and rose again from the dead."[2]

WHY IT MATTERS SO MUCH

When Jesus rose from the dead on that first Easter morning, everything changed. He had taken our sins to the cross and to the grave, and He did it to bring us victory. If Jesus had not risen from the dead, our faith would have no meaning.

Colossians 2 tells us that we were dead in our sins, but Jesus made us alive together with Him, wiped out the handwriting of the lists against us, and nailed them to the cross. The acts of His death and resurrection cancelled the charges against us. We can celebrate because all the sins we have ever committed, including our intrinsic sin nature, are nailed to the cross.

Remember the sign the Romans had posted on the cross over Jesus' head, "THIS IS JESUS THE KING OF THE JEWS"? Usually the placard gave the name and the crime for which the person was being crucified so people would see it and avoid getting into trouble with Rome for doing the same thing. But they couldn't come up with any sins that Jesus had committed. He was the pure, unstained Lamb of God. That's why He was able to die for our sins. His resurrection proves that He defeated sin and all its power. When He walked out of the tomb that day, His act wrote "forgiven" over all our sins. Talk about winning. "Having disarmed principalities and powers, He made a public spectacle of them, triumphing over them in it" (Col. 2:15).

Paul summarized the whole thing in 1 Corinthians 15, the great resurrection chapter. Dr. Gary Habermas noted that the record in this chapter points back to the AD 30s and calls up material from early eyewitnesses; Jesus appeared to groups and to individuals, including the skeptic James. First, Paul reminded his readers of what they were to hold on to: "I delivered to you first of all that which I also received: that Christ died for our sins according to the Scriptures, and that He was buried, and that He rose again the third day according to the Scriptures" (1 Cor. 15:3–4). Paul reminded them this was all verified by the appearances of the risen Lord.

But Paul admitted some don't believe in resurrection, not of Jesus and not of anyone else. He agreed that if there is no such thing as resurrection, then Jesus is not resurrected. Pointedly, Paul said, "And if Christ is not risen, then our preaching is empty and your faith is also empty" (1 Cor. 15:14). It's all nothing without the resurrection of Jesus. "And if Christ is not risen, your faith is futile; you are still in your sins!" (1 Cor. 15:17). And if that's true, we believers are to be pitied most of all. Our faith would be built on a tissue of lies.

But Paul, writing under the direction of God the Holy Spirit, asserted that without a doubt, "Now Christ is risen from the dead" (1 Cor. 15:20). He finished this powerful chapter with the renowned words, "Death is swallowed up in victory" (1 Cor. 15:54), and "Thanks be to God, who gives us the victory through our Lord Jesus Christ" (1 Cor. 15:57).

Why It Matters So Much to You

The death and resurrection of Jesus are solid history but not dry history. They offer you and me a basis for living. Jesus' death and resurrection were His main mission. He was God the Son, and He came to Bethlehem to go to Calvary, to accomplish for us what we couldn't accomplish for ourselves—to pay the debt for sin that we couldn't pay. His mission is validated by the fact that He walked out of the tomb in victory.

Now He invites us to walk in newness of life. He invites us to step away from the cross and the empty tomb with Him and walk into a life of purpose, into a life of peace regardless of the storms that come our way, into a life of contentment whether we have much or little, into a way of life where His radical love flows through us to others. He invites us to be real with Him and leave hypocrisy behind; He invites us to overcome temptation in His strength and by His Word; He invites us into a worship experience that is reverent and authentic. He comforts us by assuring us that He is continually praying for us. Does this sound like the kind of life you want?

The 1,000-day ministry of Jesus that we have traced points to His death and resurrection. His resurrection is the triumphant climax of His work on the cross. The final message of His ministry was written in actions, not words. The message is this: Jesus wins!

What can we do to make it ours? We can start with a few actions of our own.

Say thank you. Just offer a simple prayer of gratitude to Jesus for what He did on the cross and for walking out of the tomb. He never gets tired of hearing His children say thank you.

Begin today, if you are not already on the way, to live the resurrection way. Whether you are a new or experienced believer, start today to claim His resurrection power to live the way He did, modeled during His 1,000-day ministry.

Look in the mirror and say, "Jesus wins and I'm on His side, so I'm a winner!" Choose to believe it. Regardless of what your background or current circumstances are telling you, the bottom-line truth is that you are a winner in Jesus.

Pick particular fruits of the spirit to focus on. What do you need most—love, joy, peace, goodness, kindness, patience, faithfulness, gentleness, or self-control? Take one fruit at a time and ask Jesus to grow and ripen it in your life, in your interactions with others, starting now.

If you blow it—and you will from time to time—remember His promises to forgive, and start over.

The story is told of a missionary who went to a remote island in the South Pacific and began telling people about Jesus. When they heard the story, several islanders said, "Oh, this Jesus used to live here." The missionary didn't understand what they meant until he discovered that years before, another missionary had come to the island to tell about Jesus. He had lived in the midst of the people in such a way that when the islanders were later told again the Jesus story and what His life was like, they thought the earlier missionary they had heard about must have been Jesus Himself.

You, too, can live the Jesus-life. You can do it, not because you are able but because He is able and He is with you and in you. Stand up where you are right now. Take a step with your foot. Just so, take a soul-step into living the life Jesus modeled for us. Maybe your first step will be to smile at the first person you meet, say hello to your neighbor, forgive your boss, let it go when someone cuts you off in traffic, express patience to a child, inhale Jesus' peace into your present trial, claim self-control in temptation, persevere in reading your Bible daily, stay in your marriage for one more day, share an element of your faith with a friend, find fulfillment in the task at hand, or trade your aching heart for a moment of deep joy and then another moment. Picture Jesus in your shoes, and walk the way He would walk.

It is profoundly simple because it is not about patterning your life after a fine life; it is about letting the victorious Jesus inhabit you and express Himself through you.

Let the 1,000-day ministry of Jesus chart the route and set the pace for your next 1,000 days. All you need to do is take the first step. Maybe you, too, will be mistaken for Jesus.

QUESTIONS FOR INDIVIDUAL REFLECTION
OR SMALL GROUP DISCUSSION

1. Talk about what it means to be victorious. What does it mean when Jonathan writes that because Jesus wins, we win too?
2. If Jesus had never risen from the dead, where would that leave us? Discuss.
3. What are some of the ways people try to explain away the resurrection as just a natural occurrence?
4. What are some of the proofs of Jesus' resurrection?
5. How does the resurrection of Jesus give us power to live as Jesus lived?

Chapter 1: When You Want Something More

1. St. Augustine, *Confessions* (Clark, 1876).

Chapter 2: Jesus Close-Up

1. "Turn Your Eyes upon Jesus" by Helen H. Lemmel, Copyright Singspiration 1922, renewal 1950.

Chapter 4: The Offer: Supreme Happiness

1. Their story is told in William Anderson, *Angel of Hudson Bay* (Toronto: Clarke, Irwin & Company Ltd., 1961).

Chapter 6: The Way of Radical Love

1. Charles Dickens, *A Tale of Two Cities* (Whitefish, MT: Kessinger, 2004), 379.

Chapter 8: The Paradoxical Happiness of *Less*

1. Cynthia Littleton, "Sheen Returning to 'Two and a Half Men,'" *Variety*, May 17, 2010, http://www.variety.com/article/VR1118019521.

Chapter 10: When Temptation Meets Endurance

1. Dr. J. Vernon McGee, *Thru the Bible with J. Vernon McGee*, vol. 4 (Pasadena, CA: Thru The Bible Radio, 1983), 22.

Chapter 12: Peace—Now

1. Richard J. Maybury, *U.S. & World Early Warning Report*, Phoenix, AZ: Henry Madison Research, Inc., 2011, January 2011, 4.
2. Millie Stamm, *Be Still and Know* (Grand Rapids: Zondervan, 1978), preface.

Chapter 13: When Jesus Prays for You

1. Jim McKinnon, "The phone line from Flight 93 was still open when a GTE operator heard Todd Beamer say: 'Are you guys ready? Let's roll,'" *Pittsburgh Post-Gazette*, September 16, 2001, http://www.post-gazette.com/headlines/20010916phonecallnat3p3.asp.

Chapter 14: Seven Messages from the Cross

1. Peter Steinfels, *The New York Times*, March 26, 2005; and Richard Young, quoting Kelly Clem, *Echoes from Calvary* (Lanham, MD: Rowman and Littlefield, 2005), 87.

2. Laura Hillenbrand, *Unbroken: A World War II Story of Survival, Resilience, and Redemption* (New York: Random House, 2010).

Chapter 15: The Loudest Sermon Ever

1. www.solagroup.org/articles/christianliving/cl_0001.html, accessed August 2011.

2. Ibid.

BIBLE STUDY GUIDE

(with Leader's Helps)

T hanks for reading this book. I hope you have enjoyed it and that you have grown closer to Jesus during this time. I have included some discussion questions and going-deeper ideas because I want to help you think and talk through the ideas presented. You can use this section alone or in a group.

Each of the next fifteen studies is subdivided into helpful sections with opening discussion questions, passages of Scripture to read, study questions, items to pray about, a passage of Scripture to memorize, specific ways you can serve others, and topics for further study. I encourage you to work through every item in the study, yet feel free to adapt this study to your individual or group's needs.

If you are a group leader, some quick reminders:

- Encourage everyone to individually read through all of *1,000 Days.* You might want to have them do this all at once before you start the study or a chapter each week. Stay open to whatever questions the group members have as a result of interacting with the content.
- Go to the Scriptures together whenever various questions and opinions come up. Look for God's answers and perspectives. Use the Bible to help keep God in charge of your discussion.
- Set an example by responding honestly to the themes of *1,000 Days.* All of us have a lot of room to grow in learning how to live out this book's ideas. So be candid about your personal needs. As you face your group honestly, you will be encouraging others in your group to do the same.

- Pray with and for your group members. Ask God to be at work in their lives, and thank Him ahead of time (by faith) for what He will do.
- As you pray, ask God to protect your group from disunity, selfishness, and pride. Ask the Holy Spirit to give all of you spiritual insight into His truths from the Bible. Ask for the personal discoveries and breakthroughs that are most needed in each person's life.

Dig deeper at trbc.org/1000days.

CHAPTER 1: WHEN YOU WANT SOMETHING MORE

Topic: Restless Hearts Meet the Peace of Jesus

Passages: John 1; 1 John 5:11–13

Open: Talk about anything that needs to change in your life. How satisfied with life are you right now? What's the basis for your satisfaction (or lack of it)?

Read: John 1:1–32

Discuss:

1. Who is "the Word" talked about in John 1:1, and what characteristics of "the Word" are noted in John 1:1–3?
2. According to John 1:6–9, 15, 19–34, what was John the Baptist's role in Jesus' life?
3. What did the gospel writer mean when he wrote, "The Word became flesh and made his dwelling among us" (John 1:14 NIV)?
4. Read John 1:16. What are the "blessings" talked about in this verse, and how does a person receive them?
5. How does Jesus answer the longings of a restless heart?

Prayer:

- Pray that you would grow closer to God as you study Scripture.
- Pray that you would know the peace that God gives in your heart.
- Spend some time thanking God for sending Jesus.

Memorize/Meditate:

This week read this verse out loud five times daily, and think about its meaning: "He who has the Son has life; he who does not have the Son of God does not have life" (1 John 5:12 NIV).

Obey/Serve:

- Commit yourself to studying the Bible throughout the course of this guide.
- Take a walk through your neighborhood, and pray for the families in each house or apartment.

For Further Study:

Read 1 John 5:11–13, and discuss the confidence you can have in knowing Christ. In your most honest moments, where are you spiritually right now, and where do you want to be? Take some time to journal your thoughts.

CHAPTER 2: JESUS CLOSE-UP

Topic: Listening to God's Word

Passages: Luke 4; Isaiah 42; 58; 61

Open: Who was your favorite teacher in school and why?

Read: Luke 4:16–30

Discuss:

1. What are some of the ideas people have for what Jesus' mission on earth was?
2. According to this story, what was Jesus' reason for coming to earth?
3. Read the Isaiah passages Jesus read in the synagogue: Isaiah 42:6–7; 58:6–7; 61. Why did Jesus stop and not read past Isaiah 61:5?
4. What was the reaction of the audience to Jesus' teaching? Why do you think they reacted that way?
5. How would you have felt if you were in the synagogue, hearing this hometown teacher teach? How would you have reacted?
6. Grade yourself on how you interact with God's Word in these areas. Which ones are easiest for you? Which ones are hardest? Why?

   a. Listening
   b. Studying
   c. Memorizing/Meditating
   d. Practicing

7. Honestly, do you ever struggle to pay attention in Sunday services? Discuss which of these might help you listen better:

   a. Shut down early the night before the service, and be sure to get plenty of rest. Clear your mind of the distraction of late-night movies, Internet surfing, etc., and prepare yourself to hear from God.
   b. Bring a Bible and pen with you. Prepare to open to the passage the pastor is teaching from, and be ready to write down a thought, question, or important point that will keep you focused.
   c. Sit where you will be most dialed in, where you won't be

distracted. This may include deciding whom you sit with! If their presence or talking disrupts your attention, sit elsewhere.

Prayer:

Pray with your group about this lesson and the group's needs.

Memorize/Meditate:

This week read this verse out loud five times daily, and think about its meaning: "Therefore everyone who hears these words of mine and puts them into practice is like a wise man who built his house on the rock" (Matt. 7:24 NIV).

Obey/Serve:

- Are you regularly reading the written Word of God?
- Will you commit to listening to, studying, meditating on, and practicing Scripture? If not, what's holding you back?
- Will you commit to do the same with Jesus? As you read about Him during this series, will you be a faithful follower of the Living Word?

For Further Study:

Here are some steps you and your group can take to better study God's Word:

1. Pray. Ask the Holy Spirit to guide your study. He lives in each of you, He wrote the Bible, He makes it come alive for you, and He will teach you (John 14:26; 1 Cor. 3:16; 2 Peter 1:21).
2. Read. Choose a paragraph, story, or chapter in the Bible to read aloud, taking turns. Continue the reading each time you meet, being sure to finish the whole chapter, story, or book—don't just jump around.

3. Discuss. Talk about the passage:

  a. What is the meaning of the passage?
  b. What lessons, instructions, or commands are there?
  c. What questions or difficult issues does the passage raise?
  d. What encouragement does it offer?
  e. What picture does it give me of God? What does it teach me about Jesus?

4. Research. Together, or on your own, look at commentaries and other Bible study resources to examine what other Christians have learned about this passage.

CHAPTER 3: ORDINARY PEOPLE, EXTRAORDINARY LIVES

Topic: An Invitation to Follow

Passages: Luke 5; 8

Open: What have been some of the major intersections of your life? Describe a time that you had to choose to go in a new direction. How did going through this time make you feel?

Read: Luke 5:1–11, 27–32

Discuss:

1. Talk through the different disciples in this story. What did each of them have to leave to follow Jesus? What might have been going through their minds as they made the choice to follow?
2. Why do you think people in our time and culture have a hard time following Christ? Is it because of fear? Insecurity? Pride? Ignorance? The challenge?

3. There's a special group of disciples that we often forget about. Read about them in Luke 8:1–3; 23:49, 53–56.

   a. Why do you think they chose to follow Jesus?

   b. How would you describe their commitment to follow Christ? What did they do for Jesus?

4. Can you give an example of a time when Jesus has asked you for the types of obedience we read in the story? How did you handle the decision?

   a. "Can I use your boat?"—simple obedience.

   b. "Go out and fish"—challenging obedience.

   c. "Drop it all and follow Me"—total obedience.

5. What is the next step of obedience you need to take in following Jesus? What is something you might have to "drop"?

Prayer:

- Pray for the specific needs of your group.
- Pray that each of you will take the next steps of obedience with Jesus.
- Pray for your neighbors and friends who don't know Christ.

Memorize/Meditate:

This week read this verse out loud five times daily, and think about its meaning: "If anyone would come after me, he must deny himself and take up his cross daily and follow me" (Luke 9:23 NIV).

Obey/Serve:

- Make a list of the next steps you could take to follow Christ in the next thirty days. Share it with someone in your group.

- Take a walk through your neighborhood, and pray for the families in each house or apartment.

For Further Study:

1. To find out about the first day some of the disciples met Jesus, read John 1:35–51.
2. Read Luke 6:12–16 for a list of the twelve apostles. Research their lives.

CHAPTER 4: THE OFFER: SUPREME HAPPINESS

Topic: Life in Jesus' Kingdom

Passage: Matthew 5:1–12

Open: If you were the leader of your country, what is the one law you would put into motion? What is the top law you would repeal?

Read: Matthew 5:1–12

Discuss:

1. Colossians 1:13 says we are citizens in God's kingdom. Ask some of your group members to share a quick account of how they entered God's kingdom—in other words, how they became a Christian.
2. Every kingdom or nation has laws and codes of behavior it expects from its citizens. In the same way, Jesus talked much about how people who are citizens of His kingdom should behave. Matthew 5–7 gives us a great example of this teaching. Look at the first twelve verses, the "Beatitudes," and answer these questions:

a. What is the meaning of each beatitude?

b. Which ones are easier for you to practice? Which ones are harder?

- "Blessed are the poor in spirit, for theirs is the kingdom of heaven."
- "Blessed are those who mourn, for they shall be comforted."
- "Blessed are the meek, for they shall inherit the earth."
- "Blessed are those who hunger and thirst for righteousness, for they shall be filled."
- "Blessed are the merciful, for they shall obtain mercy."
- "Blessed are the pure in heart, for they shall see God."
- "Blessed are the peacemakers, for they shall be called sons of God."
- "Blessed are those who are persecuted for righteousness' sake, for theirs is the kingdom of heaven."

3. What would it look like to have a community actually live out these eight codes? What would it look like if a church practiced these?

4. What are some ways your group could practice living out the Beatitudes this month?

Prayer:

- Pray for the specific needs of your group.
- Ask God for wisdom and discipline to live out the eight Beatitudes this week.
- Pray for your neighbors and friends who don't know Christ.

Memorize/Meditate:

This week read this verse out loud five times daily, and think about its meaning: "He has delivered us from the power of darkness and conveyed us into the kingdom of the Son of His love" (Col. 1:13).

Obey/Serve:

- Make a list of how you will practice the Beatitudes this month. Share it with someone in your group.
- Take a walk through your neighborhood, and pray for the families in each house or apartment.

For Further Study:

Read more about the differences between Christ's kingdom and the kingdom of darkness. Contrast the behaviors (Gal. 5:19–23).

CHAPTER 5: SMOOTH SAILING VERSUS CALMED STORM

Topic: True Discipleship

Passage: Matthew 8:18–27

Open: What are some of the false beliefs people have surrounding what it means to be a Christian?

Read: Matthew 8:18–22

Discuss:

1. What comes to mind when you read these verses? Do you think that Jesus is being unrealistic or expecting too much? What does He really want?
2. Think about Jesus' words here in today's world. Are they harder for North Americans to accept than people from Third World nations? Are there differences in how the generations receive these words—teenagers, young adults, parents, grandparents? Why?

3. Do you think people feel that they deserve something or life gets easier and problems go away when they become a Christian? Why do we get this way?

4. Read Matthew 8:23–27. Jonathan's father, Dr. Jerry Falwell, often said, "Your greatest opportunities are often disguised as your greatest obstacles." What is typically your first response when difficulties come? Why do you think many people tend to blame God or turn their backs on Him when challenges and obstacles come?

5. It says that even the wind and the waves obey Him. How has Jesus carried you through the storms of life? What has He done to help you when following Him became difficult?

Prayer:

- Pray for the specific needs of your group—specifically, are there any "storms" any of you are going through?
- Ask God for the commitment to live a surrendered life to Christ.
- Pray for your neighbors and friends who don't know Christ.

Memorize/Meditate:

This week read this verse out loud five times daily, and think about its meaning: "In the same way, any of you who does not give up everything he has cannot be my disciple" (Luke 14:33 NIV).

Obey/Serve:

- Make a list of the things you still need to offer up to Christ's leadership and lordship in your life. Share it with someone in your group, and commit these to prayer.
- Take a walk through your neighborhood, and pray for the families in each house or apartment.

For Further Study:

Read more about how Jesus described discipleship (Luke 14:25–33). What do these characteristics mean? How do they look lived out in our culture today?

CHAPTER 6: THE WAY OF RADICAL LOVE

Topic: Loving Your Neighbor

Passages: Matthew 25:31–46; Luke 10:29–37

Open: Give an example of a time someone went above and beyond the call of duty to help you out.

Read: Luke 10:29–37; Matthew 25:31–46

Discuss:

1. Look back over Luke 10:29–37. Why did the priest, Levite, and Samaritan act the way they did? What was their motivation? Do you understand why they did what they did?
2. Which of the characters in this story do you identify most with today? Whose shoes are you in?
3. What are the barriers to loving your neighbor? Why is it challenging to do?
4. Thinking about the five steps the Samaritan took to "love his neighbor," which of these best represents where you are presently?

    a. "Leave home": I am taking simple steps to serve in my church.
    b. "Travel the road": I am living my life around hurting people, those in need; I know them by name.

    c. "Open your eyes": I pray and ask God to show me the needs of others regularly.

    d. "Open your bag": I maintain margins in my time and resources so I can be generous to help others.

    e. "Go the distance": I am living sacrificially to serve others.

5. What could you do as a group to become more loving to your neighbors?

Prayer:

- Pray for the specific needs of your group.
- Pray for your neighbors and friends who don't know Christ.

Memorize/Meditate:

This week read this verse out loud five times daily, and think about its meaning: "'Love the Lord your God with all your heart and with all your soul and with all your strength and with all your mind'; and, 'Love your neighbor as yourself'" (Luke 10:27 NIV).

Obey/Serve:

- Make a list of ways you could "love your neighbor." Start serving them this week.
- Take a walk through your neighborhood, and pray for the families in each house or apartment.

For Further Study:

Read more about how Jesus feels about serving and loving our neighbors.

Look at Matthew 25:31–46. What were the actions of those who were judged and those who were blessed?

CHAPTER 7: THE JAILS OF HYPOCRISY

Topic: Hypocrisy

Passage: Luke 11:37–54

Open: What one person has had the most positive impact on you spiritually and why?

Read: Luke 11:37–54

Discuss:

1. The meaning of the word *Pharisee* is "separatist" or "separated one." How is this Pharisee showing that he is a "separated one" in his dealing with Jesus (v. 38)?
2. Have you ever judged someone negatively because they didn't do something the way you did it? Why do you think we do this? (Hint: It starts with a *P* and rhymes with "ride.")
3. Why do we tend to "feel better" when we judge someone in a negative light? Discuss.
4. How many "woes" does Jesus pronounce on the Pharisees? Create a list of the different "woes" that Jesus pronounced on the Pharisees. Why do you think He was so harsh on this group of people?
5. In your own words, what is a hypocrite?
6. Here are seven characteristics of a hypocrite from this passage:

   a. Prefers the letter of the Law over the spirit—verse 42
   b. Wants the prominent seat (recognition)—verse 43
   c. Prefers dead rules over living truth—verse 44
   d. Has a do-as-I-say-not-as-I-do attitude—verses 45–46
   e. Tolerates other blasphemers—verses 47–51
   f. Confuses God's Word on purpose—verse 52
   g. Wails and complains when confronted—verses 53–54

7. Around the room, are there one or two of the above that you have struggled with in the past or are currently struggling with now?

8. Read verses 34–36. How does "purity of heart" help prevent hypocrisy in our lives? Let's create some suggestions to have a purer heart.

Prayer:

- Pray for the specific needs of your group. Specifically, how can we overcome hypocrisy when we have pride in our own lives?
- Ask God for the commitment to live a surrendered life to Christ.
- Pray for your neighbors and friends who don't know Christ.

Memorize/Meditate:

This week read this verse out loud five times daily, and think about its meaning: "These people draw near to Me with their mouth, and honor Me with their lips, but their heart is far from Me" (Matt. 15:8).

Obey/Serve:

- Make sure you are not being hypocritical in your dealings with others.
- Take a walk through your neighborhood, and pray for the families in each house or apartment.

For Further Study:

Meditate on what it means to first take out the plank in your own eye before you attempt to remove the speck from your brother's eye (Matt. 7:5).

CHAPTER 8: THE PARADOXICAL HAPPINESS OF *LESS*

Topic: The Tension in Wanting Stuff

Passage: Luke 12:13–21

Open: What was your first car and how did you come to own it? And if you could own any type of vehicle in the world, what vehicle would you choose?

Read: Luke 12:13–21

Discuss:

1. According to verse 13, what challenge was Jesus faced with? How did He answer the question in verses 14–15? Why do you think He warned this man about greed in this context?
2. Could someone please summarize the parable, in your own words, that Jesus gave in Luke 12:16–20?
3. Could someone else rework the parable into a modern-day example? Maybe a couple of people.
4. What is one area that you struggle with in regard to possessions? Go around the room. (Possible answers could include clothes, technology, furniture, cars, houses, or all of the above.)
5. In the context of this story, what does a "fool" look like?
6. Read Matthew 6:19–21. What is Jesus' recommendation regarding investments?
7. What happens to our hearts when we start investing in kingdom priorities? On a scale of 1 to 10, where is your heart in relation to the kingdom (1 being indifferent to 10 being focused)?
8. Let's create a list of ways that we can make kingdom of heaven investments. (Go around the room.)

Prayer:

- Pray for the specific needs of your group. Specifically, how can we overcome materialism when we live in a world surrounded by materialism?
- Ask God for the commitment to live a surrendered life to Christ.
- Pray for your neighbors and friends who don't know Christ.

Memorize/Meditate:

This week read this verse out loud five times daily, and think about its meaning: "No one can serve two masters; for either he will hate the one and love the other, or else he will be loyal to the one and despise the other. You cannot serve God and mammon" (Matt. 6:24).

Obey/Serve:

- Make a list of the things you still need to offer up to Christ's leadership and lordship in your life. Share it with someone in your group, and commit these to prayer.
- Take a walk through your neighborhood, and pray for the families in each house or apartment.

For Further Study:

Compare Luke 12 to Matthew 6 and note the similarities and the differences.

CHAPTER 9: GOOD NEWS/BAD NEWS

Topic: Jesus' Teaching on Heaven and Hell

Passage: Luke 16:19–31

Open: If your house was burning down, what three objects would you try to save?

Read: Luke 16:19–31

Discuss:

1. Could someone try to rephrase this story using a modern-day illustration?
2. If there were a moral to this story, what would it be?
3. Have you ever heard the expression, "An ounce of prevention is worth a pound of cure"? What do you think it means in this context?
4. Let's look at Matthew 13:41–43. This passage makes it clear there are two destinations after this life. What are they?
5. Everyone ends up somewhere, but few people end up somewhere on purpose. According to Romans 10:9–10, how do you make heaven your destination?
6. According to 2 Thessalonians 1:7–10, what happens to people who don't know God at the coming of Jesus Christ?
7. When did you change your default destination from hell to heaven? Go around the room and share your story.
8. In John 14:1–6, Jesus describes some things about heaven. What do you think will be the best part about heaven?

Prayer:

- Pray for the individual needs of your group—specifically, not only how we can prepare now to make heaven our destination, but how we can hear from God, "Well done, good and faithful servant."
- Ask God for the commitment to live a surrendered life to Christ.
- Pray for your neighbors and friends who don't know Christ.

Memorize/Meditate:

This week read this verse out loud five times daily, and think about its meaning: "Not everyone who says to me, 'Lord, Lord,' will enter the kingdom of heaven, but only he who does the will of my Father who is in heaven" (Matt. 7:21 NIV).

Obey/Serve:

- Make a list of the things you still need to offer up to Christ's leadership and lordship in your life. Share it with someone in your group and commit these to prayer.
- Take a walk through your neighborhood, and pray for the families in each house or apartment.

For Further Study:

Create a list of the glories of heaven and compare them with the agonies of hell.

CHAPTER 10: WHEN TEMPTATION MEETS ENDURANCE

Topic: Jesus' Teaching on Temptation

Passage: Luke 4:1–13

Open: Give three words to describe how you feel right now and what God has been teaching you lately.

Read: Luke 16:19–31

Discuss:

1. According to this passage, who led Jesus into the wilderness to be tempted by God?

2. Does God tempt people toward evil? Refer to James 1:12–15.

3. What is the longest you have gone without food? (Go around the room.) How long did Jesus go without food in this story?

4. What is the first temptation? How did Jesus handle the first temptation (Luke 4:4)?

5. What is the second temptation? How did Jesus handle the second temptation?

6. What is the third temptation? How did Jesus respond to this temptation? Based on this account, how should we respond to temptation?

7. How is the temptation of Jesus like the temptation of Adam and Eve in Genesis 3?

8. What categories of temptation do we see in 1 John 2:15–17?

9. From the three categories in 1 John 2:15–17, what area do you struggle with the most?

Prayer:

- Pray for the specific needs of your group—specifically, how we can resist temptation.
- Ask God for the commitment to live a surrendered life to Christ.
- Pray for your neighbors and friends who don't know Christ.

Memorize/Meditate:

This week read these verses out loud five times daily, and think about their meaning: "But each person is tempted when they are dragged away by their own evil desire and enticed. Then, after desire has conceived, it gives birth to sin; and sin, when it is full-grown, gives birth to death" (James 1:14–15 NIV).

Obey/Serve:

- Make a list of the things you still need to offer up to Christ's leadership and lordship in your life. Share it with someone in your group, and commit these to prayer.

- Take a walk through your neighborhood, and pray for the families in each house or apartment.

For Further Study:

Compare and contrast Luke 4 with Genesis 3 and 1 John 2:15–17, and note the similarities in the process of temptation.

CHAPTER 11: BEYOND THE HYPE

Topic: Jesus' Teaching on Worship

Passage: Luke 19:35–40

Open: What is the first thing that comes to mind when you think about God?

Read: Luke 19:35–40

Discuss:

1. What were the disciples proclaiming about Jesus as He entered Jerusalem?
2. On the basis of this proclamation, what did they think about the identity of Jesus? Refer to Matthew 16:13–16.
3. When did Jesus become more than a concept to you? Put another way, when did Jesus become your Lord and Savior? Refer to Romans 10:9–10.
4. How did the Pharisees respond? Why do you think they responded this way?
5. What was Jesus' response to the Pharisees?
6. What comes to mind when you think of worship?

7. Take a look at John 4:1–26. How does Jesus explain worship at the end of this conversation?

8. Last week we looked at the temptation of Christ and the devil wanting Jesus to worship him. What did that worship look like in Matthew 4:9?

9. To you, what does it mean to worship God in "spirit" and "truth"?

10. What are some ways we can express our worship to God? (Go around the room.)

Prayer:

- Pray for the individual needs of your group—specifically, how we can worship God right now.
- Ask God for the commitment to live a surrendered life to Christ.
- Pray for your neighbors and friends who don't know Christ.

Memorize/Meditate:

This week read this verse out loud five times daily, and think about its meaning: "Who shall not fear You, O Lord, and glorify Your name? For You alone are holy. For all nations shall come and worship before You, for Your judgments have been manifested" (Rev. 15:4).

Obey/Serve:

- Make a list of some different ways we can express worship to God.
- Take a walk through your neighborhood, and pray for the families in each house or apartment.

For Further Study:

Do a word study of *worship* and note how many times the word is used in the Bible and how many different ways people have expressed worship to God.

CHAPTER 12: PEACE—NOW

Topic: Perfect Peace

Passage: John 14:1–3

Open: Think back to your childhood, and talk about a time when you were scared.

Read: Luke 19:35–40

Discuss:

1. Read John 13:31–38. Jesus had just told the disciples He was going to be leaving them. What do you think the disciples might have been feeling and thinking as they heard Jesus' words that day?
2. In John 14:1–4 Jesus uses words that describe the engagement of a young Jewish couple. Why is this a great analogy for helping us have "perfect peace"?
3. Read Colossians 1:19–20 and Romans 5:1. What is the difference between being at peace "with" God and experiencing the peace "of" God?
4. In John 14:27 Jesus said, "Peace I leave with you; my peace I give you. I do not give to you as the world gives. Do not let your hearts be troubled and do not be afraid" (NIV). How is the peace in a believer's life different from that of the world?
5. As you think about your life right now, where are you having a hard time trusting God?
6. Read Romans 15:13. What part of that verse most speaks to you? Why?

Prayer:

Spend your time praying for the worries and burdens that people in your group are carrying.

Memorize/Meditate:

This week read this verse out loud five times daily, and think about its meaning: "And the peace of God, which transcends all understanding, will guard your hearts and your minds in Christ Jesus" (Phil. 4:7 NIV).

Obey/Serve:

- This week when you feel yourself begin to worry, quietly pray your "Declaration of Dependence" with the words, "Lord, I trust You."
- If you are having trouble trusting God, you might want to write out a list of the things that are causing you to be worried and anxious. One by one surrender your list to God, and declare your desire to trust Him.

For Further Study:

Read and reflect on Psalm 23. This psalm is most often used at a funeral, but it is a wonderful passage for helping us learn to trust God and experience His perfect peace.

CHAPTER 13: WHEN JESUS PRAYS FOR YOU

Topic: The Fruitful Life

Passage: John 15:1–5, 17

Open: What is the most festive occasion or best party you have ever attended?

Read: John 15:1–5, 17

Discuss:

1. In John 15:4 Jesus said, "Abide in Me, and I in you." In your everyday life, what does it look like practically for you to "abide in Christ"?
2. In John 15:5 Jesus said, "He who abides in Me, and I in him, bears much fruit." Make a list of the specific kinds of fruit that a Christ-follower should bear. Find some verses that give examples of spiritual "fruit."
3. In John 17:11, Jesus prayed for our unity. What is biblical "unity"? What is the difference between unity and uniformity?
4. What are some practical ways that we as believers can promote and protect unity within the body of Christ?
5. In John 17:15, Jesus prayed that we would be "in" the world but not "of" the world. Read Romans 12:2 and 1 John 2:15–17. In general, what are some areas where Christians in our generation need to be more separate from the world?
6. In John 17:17, Jesus prayed that we would be sanctified by the truth. Practically speaking, what does it mean to be "sanctified by the truth"? See 2 Timothy 3:16–17 for some help with this question.

Prayer:

- Based on John 17:11 pray for the unity of your group and for the unity of your church.
- Also spend time praying that your group would not be "of" the world, but would be on mission "in" the world.

Memorize/Meditate:

This week read this verse out loud five times daily, and think about its meaning: "I am the vine; you are the branches. If you remain in me and I in you, you will bear much fruit; apart from me you can do nothing" (John 15:5 NIV).

Obey/Serve:

- Commit this week to use your words to promote unity rather than use words that bring division and hurt.
- Ask God to reveal any area where you are being conformed to the world. Then take whatever action is necessary to stop following the world.

For Further Study:

Read Ephesians 4:1–13. Notice all of the places in this passage where "unity" is referenced. Make a list of all the things in this passage that promote and lead to unity.

CHAPTER 14: SEVEN MESSAGES FROM THE CROSS

Topic: The Gospel of the Cross

Passages: Matthew 27; Luke 22–23; 1 Corinthians 1:18

Open: Have one or two people briefly share their story of how they came to Christ.

Read: Matthew 27; Luke 22–23; 1 Corinthians 1:18

Discuss:

1. There are six characters in the story of the cross: oblivious soldiers, hardened criminal, amazed centurion, repentant

criminal, devoted disciples, hidden disciples. Which character can you most relate to? Why?

2. Have someone read John 19:17–42 out loud for the group. As you hear this familiar story again, what most stands out to you? Why?

3. Read 1 Corinthians 1:18–25 and 2:1–5. What lessons can we learn about the gospel of the cross from these two passages?

4. Read Hebrews 10:1–12. Why is the death of Jesus on the cross the "once and for all" and final sacrifice that had to be offered?

5. In our generation, for many the cross is nothing more than a piece of jewelry, artwork, or decoration. How can we as believers make sure we never forget both the horror and the wonder of the cross?

Prayer:

Pray specifically for your family and friends who need Christ.

Memorize/Meditate:

This week read this verse out loud five times daily, and think about its meaning: "For the message of the cross is foolishness to those who are perishing, but to us who are being saved it is the power of God" (1 Cor. 1:18 NIV).

Obey/Serve:

- Write the name of a person you believe has never accepted Christ on a card that you can carry with you throughout the week.
- Pray over that name several times each day, praying that God will give you the open door to share your faith with them.
- Seek out that open door.

For Further Study:

Spend time slowly and carefully reading the biblical accounts of the crucifixion. These can be found in Matthew 26–27; Mark 14–15; Luke 22–23; and John 18–20.

CHAPTER 15: THE LOUDEST SERMON EVER

Topic: Getting Past Your Past

Passage: John 21:1–17

Open: Brainstorm a list of people in the Bible who failed and were still used by God.

Read: John 21:1–17

Discuss:

1. In Romans 8:1 Paul says, "Therefore, there is now no condemnation for those who are in Christ Jesus" (NIV). What has been your journey in accepting God's forgiveness of your past?
2. Jesus focused on His relationship with Peter. Which of the following words best describes your current love relationship with Christ: Stuck? Drifting? Growing? Lukewarm? White hot? Distant?
3. For you personally, what helps "stoke the fires" of your love for Christ? And what causes the fire to grow cold?
4. How has God used the pain of your past to help you be better equipped to serve others?
5. Three times Jesus instructs Peter to care for and feed His sheep. How can your group "care for and feed" each other?

Prayer:

- Read Paul's prayer in Ephesians 3:14–21. Then, in your own words and in your own way, use Paul's prayer to guide you in praying for one another.
- Pray for anyone in the group who might still be struggling to get over their past.

Memorize/Meditate:

This week read this verse out loud five times daily, and think about its meaning: "Therefore, there is now no condemnation for those who are in Christ Jesus" (Rom. 8:1 NIV).

Obey/Serve:

- Several times this week read and meditate on Romans 8 and Ephesians 2:1–10. Make a list of all the statements that define your identity now that you are a Christ-follower.
- Think of someone you know who is going through a time of struggle or failure. Make it a point to pray for them and do something to encourage and bless them this week.

For Further Study:

Read 2 Samuel 11–12:14 and Psalm 51. These two passages reveal the failure and restoration of King David. He is a great case study of someone who failed miserably but still ended up being used by God.

100 Main Events in Jesus' Life

Event 1

The two genealogical records of Jesus

- As recorded by Matthew (Matt. 1:1–17)
- As recorded by Luke (Luke 3:23–37)

Event 2

The three predictions preceding the birth of Jesus

- To Zacharias, concerning the birth of John (Luke 1:5–25)
- To Mary, concerning the birth of Jesus (Luke 1:26–38)
- To Joseph, concerning the purity of Mary (Matt. 1:18–25)

Event 3

The three songs of praise anticipating the birth of Jesus

- The praise of Elizabeth to Mary (Luke 1:41–45)
- The praise of Mary to God (Luke 1:46–56)
- The praise of Zacharias to God (Luke 1:57–79)

Event 4

The birth of Jesus (Luke 2:1–19)

Event 5

The worship of Jesus by the shepherds (Luke 2:8–20)

Event 6

The circumcision of Jesus (Luke 2:21–24)

Event 7

The dedication of Jesus in the temple (Luke 2:25–38)

Event 8

The worship of Jesus by the wise men (Matt. 2:1–12)

Event 9

Jesus' flight into Egypt (Matt. 2:13–23)

Event 10

Jesus' early years in Nazareth (Luke 2:39–40, 52)

Event 11

Jesus' temple visit at age twelve (Luke 2:41–50)

Event 12

Jesus' baptism (Matt. 3:13–17; Mark 1:9–11; Luke 3:21–22; John 1:32–34)

Event 13

Jesus' temptation (Matt. 4:1–11; Mark 1:12–13; Luke 4:1–13)

Event 14

The ministry of Jesus' forerunner, John the Baptist

- The maturing of John (Luke 1:80; 3:1–2)
- The message of John (Matt. 3:1–3, 8–10; Mark 1:1–2; Luke 3:4–14; 7:29–30; John 1:29–30, 35–36)
- The mantle of John (Mark 1:4, 6)

- The ministry of John (Matt. 3:5–6; Mark 1:4–5; Luke 3:3; John 1:28)
- The misunderstanding concerning John (Luke 3:15; John 1:19–26)
- The Messiah of John (Matt. 3:11–12; Mark 1:7–8; Luke 3:16–18; John 1:6–18, 27, 30)
- The attempted muzzling of John (Matt. 14:1–5; Mark 6:14–20)
- The brief misgivings by John (Matt. 11:2–6; Luke 7:19–23)
- The martyrdom of John (Matt. 14:6–12; Mark 6:21–29)
- The magnificence of John (Matt. 11:7–15; Luke 7:24–28)

Event 15

Jesus turns water into wine (John 2:1–11)

Event 16

Jesus performs His first temple cleansing (John 2:13–25)

Event 17

Jesus selects Capernaum as His northern headquarters (Matt. 4:13–16; John 2:12)

Event 18

Jesus meets with Nicodemus (John 3:1–21)

Event 19

Jesus meets with the Samaritan woman (John 4:1–42)

Event 20

Jesus conducts five preaching tours

- First tour: Matthew 4:17; Mark 1:14–15; Luke 4:14–15
- Second tour: Matthew 4:23–25; Mark 1:35–39; Luke 4:42–44
- Third tour: Matthew 9:35–38

- Fourth tour: Matthew 11:1
- Fifth tour: Luke 8:1–3

Event 21

The conversion, choosing, and commissioning of Jesus' disciples

- The conversion of His disciples

  1. Andrew and John (John 1:37–40)
  2. Simon Peter (John 1:41–42)
  3. Philip (John 1:43–45)
  4. Nathanael (John 1:46–51)
  5. Matthew (Matt. 9:9; Mark 2:14; Luke 5:27–29)

- The choosing of His disciples

  1. First call to Peter, Andrew, James, and John (Matt. 4:18–22; Mark 1:16–20; Luke 5:1–11)
  2. Final call to the Twelve (Matt. 10:1–41; Mark 3:13, 16–19; Luke 6:12–16)

- The commissioning of His followers

  1. The first followers

     a. The twelve apostles (Matt. 10:5–15; Mark 3:14–15; 6:7–13; Luke 9:1–6)
     b. The seventy disciples (Matt. 11:25–27; Luke 10:1–24)

  2. The future followers (Matt. 10:17–42; Luke 10:16, 22)

Event 22

Jesus heals a lame man at the pool of Bethesda (John 4:46–54)

Event 23

Jesus preaches His Sermon on the Mount (Matt. 5–7)

Event 24

Jesus relates the parable of the sower and seed (Matt. 13:1–23)

Event 25

Jesus preaches from Isaiah 61 in a Nazareth synagogue (Luke 4:16–30)

Event 26

Jesus heals a paralytic (Matt. 9:2–8; Mark 2:3–12; Luke 5:18–26)

Event 27

Jesus visits with Mary and Martha (Luke 10:38–42)

Event 28

Jesus discusses various key topics

- Heaven and hell (Mark 9:42–50; John 14:1–3)
- Divorce (Matt. 19:3–12; Mark 10:1–12)
- Discipleship (Matt. 16:24–26; Mark 8:34–38; Luke 9:23–26; 14:25–27)
- Last days (Luke 17:22–37)
- Church discipline (Matt. 18:15–20)

Event 29

Jesus invites the weary and burdened to come to Him (Matt. 11:28–30)

Event 30

Jesus stills a storm (Matt. 8:23–27; Mark 4:36–41; Luke 8:22–25)

Event 31

Jesus feeds the five thousand (Matt. 14:15–21; Mark 6:30–44; Luke 9:10–17; John 6:1–14)

Event 32

Jesus walks on the water (Matt. 14:22–32; Mark 6:45–52; John 6:15–21)

Event 33

Jesus delivers a Syro-Phoenician's daughter from demon possession (Matt. 15:21–28; Mark 7:24–30)

Event 34

Jesus hears Peter's great confession and promises to build the church (Matt. 16:13–23)

Event 35

Jesus meets with three would-be disciples

- First candidate: he allows his finances to disqualify him (Matt. 8:19–20; Luke 9:57–58)
- Second candidate: he allows his family to disqualify him (Matt. 8:21–22; Luke 9:59–60)
- Third candidate: he allows his friends to disqualify him (Luke 9:61–62)

Event 36

Jesus denounces key Galilean cities

- Chorazin and Bethsaida (Matt. 11:20–22; Luke 10:13)
- Capernaum (Matt. 11:23–24; Luke 10:15)

Event 37

Jesus is confronted on two occasions by the Pharisees who demand a sign

- First occasion: Matthew 12:38–42; Luke 11:29–32
- Second occasion: Matthew 16:14; Mark 8:10–12; Luke 12:34–58

Event 38

Jesus has two encounters with His family

- First encounter: Matthew 12:46–48; Mark 3:31–35; Luke 8:19–21
- Second encounter: John 7:1–10

Event 39

Jesus meets with the rich young ruler (Matt. 19:16–26; Mark 10:17–22)

Event 40

Jesus delivers the maniac of Gadara (Mark 5:1–20)

Event 41

Jesus heals a woman with an issue of blood (Matt. 9:20–22; Mark 5:25–34; Luke 8:43–48)

Event 42

Jesus raises Jairus's daughter (Matt. 9:18–19, 23–26; Mark 5:22–24, 35–43; Luke 8:41–42, 49–56)

Event 43

Jesus is transfigured (Matt. 17:1–13; Luke 9:28–36)

Event 44

Jesus delivers a demonic son (Matt. 17:14–18; Mark 9:14–29; Luke 9:38–42)

Event 45

Jesus relates the parable of the good Samaritan (Luke 10:30–37)

Event 46

Jesus relates the parables of the lost sheep, coin, and son (Luke 15:1–32)

Event 47

Jesus relates the parable of the rich man and Lazarus (Luke 16:19–31)

Event 48

Jesus forgives the woman taken in the act of adultery (John 8:1–11)

Event 49

Jesus preaches His sermon on the good shepherd and his sheep (John 10:1–21)

Event 50

Jesus heals the man born blind (John 9)

Event 51

Jesus predicts His sufferings, death, and resurrection on three important occasions

- First occasion: after hearing Peter's confession (Matt. 16:21–23; Mark 8:31–33; Luke 9:22)
- Second occasion: after the Transfiguration (Matt. 17:22–23; Mark 9:30–32; Luke 9:43–45)
- Third occasion: just prior to His final week (Matt. 20:17–19; Mark 10:32–34; Luke 18:31–34)

Event 52

Jesus raises Lazarus from the dead (John 11:1–44)

Event 53

Jesus cleanses the lepers (Luke 17:11–19)

Event 54

Jesus rebukes James and John on three occasions

- First occasion: for sectarianism (Mark 9:38–41; Luke 9:49–50)
- Second occasion: for barbarism (Luke 9:51–56)
- Third occasion: for egotism (Matt. 20:20–28; Mark 10:35–45)

Event 55

Jesus blesses little children (Matt. 19:13–15; Mark 10:13–16; Luke 18:15–17)

Event 56

Jesus heals blind Bartimaeus (Matt. 20:29–34; Mark 10:46–52; Luke 18:35–43)

Event 57

Jesus calls Zacchaeus down from a sycamore tree (Luke 19:1–10)

Event 58

Jesus is anointed by Mary of Bethany (Matt. 26:6–13; Mark 14:3–9; John 12:1–8)

Event 59

Jesus' triumphal entry into Jerusalem (Matt. 21:1–11; Mark 11:1–10; Luke 19:29–38; John 12:12–19)

Event 60

Jesus performs His second temple cleansing (Matt. 21:12–17; Mark 11:15–18; Luke 19:45–47)

Event 61

Jesus curses the fig tree (Matt. 21:18–19)

Event 62

Jesus hears the voice of His Father

- First occasion: at His baptism (Matt. 3:16–17)
- Second occasion: at His transfiguration (Matt. 17:1–5)
- Third and final occasion: after the request by some Greeks to see Jesus (John 12:20–33)

Event 63

Jesus is subjected to five confrontations by the wicked Pharisees and Sadducees

- Over His authority (Matt. 21:23–27; Mark 11:27–33; Luke 20:3–8)
- Over paying tribute to Caesar (Matt. 22:15–22; Mark 12:13–17; Luke 20:19–25)
- Over the doctrine of the resurrection (Matt. 22:23–33; Mark 12:18–27; Luke 20:27–40)
- Over the greatest commandment (Matt. 22:34–40; Mark 12:28–34)
- Over the Messiah (Matt. 22:41–46; Mark 12:35–37; Luke 20:41–44)

Event 64

Jesus utterly condemns the wicked Pharisees (Matt. 23:1–36; Mark 12:38–40; Luke 20:45–47)

Event 65

Jesus weeps over the city of Jerusalem

- First occasion: Matthew 23:37–39; Luke 13:34–35
- Second occasion: Luke 19:41–44

Event 66

Jesus commends a poor widow for her sacrificial gift (Mark 12:41–44; Luke 21:1–4)

Event 67

Jesus delivers His Mount Olivet discourse (Matt. 24–25)

Event 68

Jesus makes preparation for the Passover (Matt. 26:17–19; Mark 14:12–16; Luke 21:7–13)

Event 69

In the Upper Room, Jesus washes the disciples' feet, institutes the Lord's Supper, and announces His betrayal (Matt. 26:17–39; Mark 14:12–25; Luke 22:7–30; John 13–14)

Event 70

Jesus delivers His fruit-bearing sermon (John 15–16)

Event 71

Jesus prays His great, high priestly prayer (John 17)

Event 72

Jesus offers up three prayers in great agony in Gethsemane (Matt. 26:36–46; Mark 14:32–42; Luke 22:39–46; John 18:1–11)

Event 73

Jesus is betrayed by Judas Iscariot

- The bargain—Judas agrees to sell Jesus out for thirty pieces of silver (Matt. 26:14–16; Mark 14:10–11; Luke 22:3–6)
- The betrayal—Judas betrays Jesus in Gethsemane (Matt. 26:43–50; Luke 22:47–48; John 18:1–5)

• The bloody field—Judas returns the money and hangs himself. The thirty pieces are used to purchase a field called *the field of blood* (Matt. 27:3–10)

Event 74

Jesus restores a severed ear in Gethsemane (Matt. 26:51–56; Mark 14:47–49; Luke 22:50–51; John 18:10–11)

Event 75

Jesus is arrested in Gethsemane (John 18:10)

Event 76

Jesus is forsaken by all in Gethsemane (Matt. 26:56; Mark 14:50–52)

Event 77

Jesus suffers His unfair and illegal trials

• The Jewish, religious trials

1. The threefold travesty during these trials (the denunciation by Annas, Caiaphas, and the Sanhedrin)

   a. Christ stands before Annas (John 18:13–14, 19–23)
   b. Christ stands before Caiaphas (Matt. 26:57, 59–68; Mark 14:53–65; Luke 22:54, 63–65; John 18:24)
   c. Christ stands before the entire Sanhedrin (Matt. 27:1; Mark 15:1)

2. The twofold tragedy during those trials (the denials of Peter and death of Judas)

   a. The denials by Peter (Matt. 26:33–35, 69–73, 75; Mark 14:29–31, 54, 66–70, 72; Luke 22:31–34, 54–59, 61–62; John 13:36–38; 18:15–17, 25–27)
   b. The death of Judas (Matt. 27:3–10)

• The Roman, political trials

1. Christ stands before Pilate for the first time (Matt. 27:2, 11–14; Mark 15:25; Luke 23:1–5; John 18:28–38)
2. Christ stands before Herod Antipas (Luke 23:6–12)
3. Christ stands before Pilate for the final time (Matt. 27:15–26; Luke 15:6–15; 23:13–24; John 18:40; 19:1, 4–5, 7–15)

• The military, mockery trial

1. Christ stands before the soldiers (Matt. 27:27–31; Mark 15:16–20; John 19:2–3)

Event 78

Jesus is brutally scourged (Matt. 27:26; Mark 15:15)

Event 79

Jesus is led to Calvary

• The man of Cyrene, lifting up Jesus' cross (Matt. 27:32; Mark 15:21; Luke 23:26)
• The maidens of Jerusalem, lamenting over Jesus' cross (Luke 23:27–31)

Event 80

Jesus is crucified between two thieves (Matt. 27:32–49; Mark 15:25; Luke 23:32; John 19:16–18)

Event 81

Jesus makes seven statements while on the cross

• The first three hours (9:00 a.m. till noon)

1. First statement from the cross: "Father, forgive them; for they know not what they do" (Luke 23:34 KJV).

2. Second statement from the cross: "Verily I say unto thee, Today shalt thou be with me in paradise" (Luke 23:43 KJV).

3. Third statement from the cross: "Woman, behold thy son! . . . Behold thy mother!" (John 19:26–27 KJV).

• The final three hours (Noon till 3:00 p.m.)

1. Fourth statement from the cross: "My God, my God, why hast thou forsaken me?" (Matt. 27:46 KJV).

2. Fifth statement from the cross: "I thirst!" (John 19:28).

3. Sixth statement from the cross: "It is finished!" (John 19:30).

4. Seventh statement from the cross: "Father, into thy hands I commend my spirit" (Luke 23:46 KJV).

Event 82

Jesus dies on the cross (Matt. 27:50; Mark 15:37; Luke 23:46; John 19:30)

Event 83

Jesus' body is pierced (John 19:31–37)

Event 84

Jesus' death is accompanied by a series of miracles

• In regards to the temple: the veil is torn from top to bottom (Matt. 27:51; Mark 15:38; Luke 23:45)

• In regards to the terrain: a localized but severe earthquake occurred (Matt. 27:51)

• In regards to the tombs: a number of people were raised from the dead (Matt. 27:52–53)

Event 85

Jesus' body is claimed and prepared for burial by Joseph of

Arimathaea and Nicodemus (Matt. 27:57–59; Mark 15:42–45; Luke 23:50–52; John 19:38–40)

Event 86

Jesus' body is placed in Joseph's tomb (Matt. 27:60; Mark 15:46; Luke 23:53; John 19:41–42)

Event 87

Jesus' tomb is officially sealed (Matt. 27:62–66)

Event 88

Jesus is raised from the dead (Matt. 28:2–4; Mark 16:4; Luke 24:2; John 20:6–7)

Event 89

Jesus appears to Mary Magdalene in the garden (Mark 16:9–10; John 20:11–18)

Event 90

Jesus appears to the women returning from the tomb (Matt. 28:5–10)

Event 91

Jesus appears to two disciples on the Emmaus road (Mark 16:12–13; Luke 24:13–32)

Event 92

Jesus appears to Peter in Jerusalem (Luke 24:34; 1 Cor. 15:5)

Event 93

Jesus appears to ten of His apostles in the Upper Room (Mark 16:14; Luke 24:36–43; John 20:19–23)

Event 94

Jesus appears to eleven of His apostles in the Upper Room (John 20:19–29)

Event 95

Jesus appears to seven of His apostles by the Sea of Galilee (John 21:1–23)

Event 96

Jesus appears to the eleven and five hundred believers on Mount Tabor (Matt. 28:16–20; 1 Cor. 15:6)

Event 97

Jesus appears to His half brother James in Jerusalem (1 Cor. 15:7)

Event 98

Jesus appears to the eleven on Mount Olivet (Luke 24:44–50)

Event 99

Jesus instructs His apostles for forty days after His resurrection (Acts 1:3)

Event 100

Jesus ascends to heaven from Mount Olivet (Mark 16:19; Luke 24:51; Acts 1:9)

About the Author

Jonathan Falwell is the senior pastor at Thomas Road Baptist Church in Lynchburg, Virginia. He is the son and successor of the late Reverend Jerry Falwell and the brother of the current Liberty University chancellor, Jerry Falwell Jr.

In addition to inheriting his father's position as pastor at Thomas Road, Falwell has continued his father's weekly column *Listen America* on various websites, including *NewsMax* and *WorldNetDaily.* He hosts a weekly television show called *Main Street Today*, interviewing people from all walks of life and discussing how their belief in God has influenced and molded their lives.

Falwell earned a bachelor degree from Liberty University in 1987, a master of arts degree in religion from the Liberty Baptist Theological Seminary in 1996, and a juris doctor degree in 2005 from the Taft Law School at William Howard Taft University.

Falwell and his wife, Shari, have four children: Jonathan Jr., Jessica, Natalie, and Nicholas. They reside in Lynchburg, Virginia.

CPSIA information can be obtained at www.ICGtesting.com
Printed in the USA
LVOW041916260213

321756LV00003B/25/P